Historic
Jersey

Historic Jersey

Seeker Publishing

www.seekerpublishing.com

Written by Jeff Le Caudey

Published
by
Seeker Publishing Ltd
Units 1&2 Elms Farm
La Mare Vineyards
La Route De La Hougue Mauger
St Mary
Jersey
JE3 3BA
www.seekerpublishing.com

Seeker
Publishing & Distribution
in the Channel Islands

We acknowledge with thanks permission to reproduce
photographs supplied by various sources including:

Stuart Abraham
Axiom Design
Société Jersiaise Photographic Archive
Publishers own collection

ISBN 978-1-905095-10-0

Printed and bound by CPI Group (UK) Ltd., Croydon, CR0 4YY

CONTENTS

CHAPTER ONE
1000 - 1200

Jersey is an amazing little rock. It only covers 45 square miles but every mile is crammed with a history of intrigue, battle and incident.

If we had been able to stand on the cliffs at Les Landes around 120 millenniums ago, we might have seen a few red deer (similar in some ways to the Jersey Cow) on the rolling green plains. We might, had we existed, have noticed some rocky mounds in the distance that were to become Guernsey and Sark. All this was part of the continent and there was really nothing to see - Tourism was definitely not booming!

We will move on rapidly, past cave dwellers, past the Mammoths, pausing to take a quick look at the Neolithics of 4000 BC who, having arrived from Europe, decided to stay and become farmers, domesticating the animals and growing their food instead of killing everything that moved and robbing everything else. Moving on past Roman times we might have picked up a few coins from 43 BC, with Mark Antony proudly featured, and even some bits of pottery.

Passing through 555 AD when poor old Helier lost his head and gained a sainthood, we leap ahead to the main point, The Millennium. Actually the story of the last 1000 years must start 75 years earlier, when, in 925 AD, Rollo, the pirate chief, ruler of most of Normandy decided, at the remarkable age of eighty, to hang up his helmet and hand his Duchy to his son, William Longsword. Boys will be boys and it was not long before young William, now a Duke, had to start showing off. There were some bloody battles across Normandy and Brittany but eventually he won the day and grabbed the Channel Islands in to the bargain. Thus Jersey entered the millennium under French rule.

This situation continued for some 200 years, during which our Prince, the Duke of Normandy, beat the English at Hastings, possibly with the help of a few local lads. It is the Jersey man's tongue in cheek claim, that 'We captured England in 1066.'

There was much bickering between different religious orders at this time. Monks in Jersey were at loggerheads with the Monks at Notre Dame in Cherbourg. Eventually the Archbishop of Rouen stepped in and also stepped on the local squad demoting the Abbey to a Priory in favour of his compatriots in Cherbourg.

Around 1180, Jersey was divided into three administrations with four parishes in each, a bit complicated to say the least. Each of these was presided over by a local landowner who had paid good money for the privilege.

Their duties included the right to collect the Duke's taxes and administer the Duke's justice. Being Jersey men, it can be assumed that they would have stood to get a few perks and gain a good return for their investment. However, as the saying goes, 'power corrupts' and before long each of them were fined at the assizes by the justices from Normandy for exceeding their powers.

Two of them, Godel and La Hougue were involved in cases of maiming, whilst the other, coincidentally named Burnouf was accused of using 'ordeal by hot iron'! Ordeal by battle was also employed, not exactly the true spirit of justice perhaps.

At this time Jersey, and the other Channel Islands were, because of 1066, part of Normandy and England under Richard the Lionheart. Normandy, however, was still not part of France. This led to a lot of infighting, general mayhem and confusion, with uncle plotting against nephew and brother against brother. Skulduggery was the order of the day. A young Prince was captured and then got 'accidentally killed whilst trying to escape'!

It was at this point that France decided that enough was enough and invaded Normandy. Very soon, that Dukedom became a part of France, and the Channel Islands were handed over to the United Kingdom, mainly because France felt that they didn't have the naval power to protect them.

But it didn't end there. Twice the French changed their minds and reclaimed us, and twice Lord John, the King, got the Islands back again. Unfortunately, at one point when Lord John thought we were well and truly held by the French, he persuaded 'Eustace the Monk', a renegade monk turned pirate, to harass the Islands, which he did to such great effect that he reported back that 'He had left naught to burn'.

La Corbière.

9

CHAPTER TWO
1200 - 1300

Eventually, around 1207 we were re-established as British. It is interesting to note that later, our friendly monk, Eustace, decided to change sides. This time he attacked and captured the Islands in the name of France. He had taken advantage of the confused situation at this time, including the death of King John and the succession to the throne of nine year old Henry III, but eventually Philippe d'Aubigny, Jersey's new warden, intercepted and captured Eustace the Monk on one of his day trips and ended his little games by beheading him on his own foredeck. Once again the Channel Islands were British.

The average Jersey man is proud to be British, provided the British don't try to tell him what to do. During the civil war, the Government demanded the support of the Channel Islands. Guernsey gave it, so naturally Jersey men supported the King.

Of small build and dark haired from generations of Normans, French and just possibly some Spanish blood, the local was a hard worker but his own welfare always took priority over the needs of others. This came from the Norman heritage, and from the countless and thankless years their ancestors spent scraping a living from the soil and fighting off invaders intent on setting fire to newly harvested crops or destroying any buildings in sight.

There were taller, fair haired Islanders, no doubt due to the Saxons and Vikings who tended to pay unexpected visits intent on the usual pillage, burning, and anything else that came to mind. Jersey blood had been mixed with people from many countries, particularly the UK. A few can claim three or four generations of 'pure Jersey' on both sides, and in fact only about half the present population is actually Jersey born.

Although it is not thought that the Romans actually occupied the Island, they did visit quite frequently to collect taxes and to dispense justice. However, although their visits took place about 60 BC, and didn't actually come in this Millennium, some of their words are to be found in the Jersey patois (Norman French) and a nucleus of our legal system originates from those gallant lads from Italy. The local population will always absorb the language of an invader. 'Mon bicyclette, she is kaput' is borne out by a phrase heard in the German Occupation, 1940/45.

It was 1218, and young Henry III, a little older and a bit wiser, said something that was to affect the well being of the Islanders for many a long year. He said, in effect, 'We have no intention of altering or interfering with the administration or constitution of the Islands'. He said they should remain as instituted by his father, uncle and grandfather, King Richard.

His decision was influenced by Rector Thomas Olivier of St Helier, who had fed him the edited highlights of the constitution on a need to know basis, thus allowing our privileges to remain intact, which was a great advantage to Jersey.

There were fears in some quarters that some Islanders still supported the French. Therefore, all the leading families had to give up one of their sons to be deported to England as hostages for their families' loyalty. Some of the lads were not reunited with their folks for eight years.

The huge demand for fish, both for local consumption and export, soon had the Jersey sons of the soil, as well as the fishermen, spreading their nets far and wide, even as far as Newfoundland, in order to keep the cooking pots and their pockets well filled.

One would think that having taken hostages from the leading families, the authorities would have rested easily in their beds, but no, they still remained suspicious and used this as an excuse to confiscate property at the drop of a chapeau.

In 1223, they even brought in a law that any landowner who spent more than a week in Normandy would have his estates confiscated. The King even ordered that the Clergy, and anyone else he was uneasy about, should not be allowed to wander around near the shoreline, presumably in case they gave aid and comfort to any approaching French.

The system of Fiefs, (an area of land presided over by the Seigneur), had long been established in the Island. In the early days, the whole thing was quite benign. The people, who lived in the Fief, touched the forelock and did odd jobs for the Seigneur. Now and then, they supplied him with a few bushels of corn or the occasional sheep. He, in turn, recognized his responsibilities and looked out for them. He provided a corn mill, and dispensed advice and justice when needed. It worked well, but gradually new ways and ideas, both political and religious, began to encroach and the happy relationship turned sour. Unjust punishments, undemocratic exacting of dues and unreasonable fines, soon had the people pulling their hair out.

Once we had been established as being British, the top man in the Islands was The Warden. Under him, each Island had their own Bailiff and other officials who all answered directly to the big man. One such Warden was Otho. Otho was very busy, quite old and very broke. He was a Knight who, as the King's ambassador, was always getting sent to sort out problems worldwide. His estate was quite small and his continued absence, plus mounting expenses took their toll. The result was that his officials found devious ways and means to make the Jersey folk fork out. As he had never had time to pay them a visit and no one had even seen the chap, the Islanders soon got fed up and began to scream long and hard in the direction of Parliament. Their response came later but, in the meanwhile, the Jersey folk had something even more unpleasant to plague their woeful lives - the French!

Rumour had it that a Norman ship had sailed down the channel, proudly displaying dead dogs and dead Englishmen hanging from the rigging. This challenge was enough to set the English and French fleets at each other's throats. The French received a good hiding. Displeased at their defeat, the French avenged their discomfit by attacking the Channel Islands. The attack was vicious, savage and devastating. They desecrated and destroyed churches, burned mills, houses and food stocks, slaughtered livestock and, to their everlasting shame, they murdered fifteen hundred women and girls. A petition was sent to the King, who, it seems, was expecting an instant rebuilding programme. It explained the lack of materials for rebuilding plus the severe shortage of food. These days everyone, from the Red Cross to the Sally Army, would have been on our doorstep, arms filled with goodies. In those days we just had to rely on the King, but he did do the sensible thing. He decided to strengthen Gorey castle, so he had his men smash up the local fishermen's boats and used the wood to build a palisade. Then he sent in more troops as reinforcements who, of course, commandeered provisions from the already beleaguered Islanders.

By 1298, Parliament was receiving so many complaints and accusations of corruption amongst the officials who were running, or ruining, the Island for the Warden, that a commission of enquiry was ordered.

Unfortunately, the Warden, Otho, had friends in high places as well as on the commission. The locals stood no chance. The enquiry lasted six weeks. Every one of the complaints against corrupt officials were quickly dismissed and, just to add insult to injury, every complainant was fined for making frivolous accusations. One man, who complained that the Clerk of the Court had entered a suit incorrectly, was jailed for contempt.

The rest of this long sitting was taken up with one hundred and eighty four cases of violent assault. It seems that in those days, provided you were of some importance or standing in the community, you could get away with just about anything. The man in the street had no rights. One such, dragged a woman from her house by her hair and beat her, broke some windows, thrashed a farmer, stole a coat and battered the Vicomte's servant. He was fined a nominal amount and later became Dean!

Perhaps the most dastardly bully and scoundrel was Sir Drogo de Barentin, The Seigneur of Rozel. Drogo regularly sent his retainers out to capture women and drag them back to the Manor house for his pleasure. Some were neighbours' wives or daughters. It made no difference to him. They were all fair game. On one occasion, he sent his thugs to break into the house of a neighbour. They rifled his belongings and even killed the dog. When the poor chap complained to the Court, Drogo's bullies dragged him out, beat him up and broke both his arms.

Drogo was so powerful and feared in the district that no Jury would convict him and he was found not guilty. However, his crimes had been so blatant that the Justices decided he had to pay three hundred Livres Turnois (about £ 22) for a King's pardon.

A slightly unusual case was that of butchers being charged with selling sheep carcasses without the heads. The suspicion was that they had been selling dog's flesh as mutton. A leper, who enjoyed breaking windows and rolling people in the mud, was taken to task and, no doubt, given words of advice.

It was at this point that the Justices decided to have a go at all the Seigneurs. Who had given them the many 'rights' that they seemed to take for granted such as the ownership of any wreckage found on their bit of the beach?

They even challenged the right of the Seigneurs to hunt across their own land, declaring that hunting was a Royal sport and no one could indulge without the King's permission, even in their own back yard. The Seigneur of St Ouen came in for some stick because he owned private gallows, and another was questioned about hunting rabbits on Town Hill. It really was a typical exercise in harassment.

The Seigneurs got very hot under the collar about all this interference, but were not really powerful enough to 'throw down the gauntlet'. In the event, they didn't even need to drop a mitten, as the Government, ever aware of possible further conflict with the French and rather wanting to keep Jersey on their side, quietly and tactfully let the matter drop, - for the moment!

There was always some Government whiz kid who would try to make a name for himself by having a go at the Channel Islands and, nine years later they went through the exact same farce again, challenging the Seigneurs on every silly little thing their devious brains could contrive. Again, after causing maximum upset, they conveniently forgot the whole thing. All they had succeeded in doing was to stir up anti-Government feelings again.

Typical country scene.

CHAPTER THREE
1300 - 1400

Edward II put on the Royal hat in 1307. He was christened 'Edward the Poltroon' by his loving subjects. In Jersey though, Sir Otho the Warden and his cohorts, were still busily engaged in trying to squeeze Jersey dry.

Again, the Islanders complained long and loudly to the new King. So he set up another Assizes full of Justices who, as you read earlier, were more interested in aggravating the gentry.

They did, of course, deal with the usual number of unusual cases. The man who cut off the tail of a lady's donkey was fined. He may also have been bound over to keep the peace. There was the pillory for giving short measures. Also, there was the macabre story of the Rector of St Brelade who, in a dawn raid, stole the corpse of a woman in a dispute over a burial.

One of the main bones of contention was the trouble brewing between the Civil and the Ecclesiastical courts. Because of the confused and lawless situation that had reigned a couple of centuries previously, the Clergy had managed to get them declared sacrosanct. This put them above the law and answerable only to the Bishop of Coutances. Everyone connected with the Church, right down to the grave-diggers, benefited from this privilege but it was a privilege with a nasty sting in its cassock.

The Civil Courts were not impressed with a system which, whilst it allowed anyone connected with the Church to be beyond civil law, these same privileged souls could, at the same time, be arrested under Ecclesiastical law, and find themselves packed off to a French prison, waiting to be sentenced by a French Bishop. Not a happy thought for a good Jersey man. Sir Otho, earning his keep for once, had a quiet word with The Pope. He saw the point and immediately issued an order scrapping this archaic practice. The King then wrote to the Bailiff and told him to get cracking, put out a proclamation, make sure that everyone knew about the new ruling, and punish anyone who tried to ignore it.

One would think that an order from the Pope, backed by the King of England would have had enough clout to settle the matter. But it didn't end there. The Bishop of Coutances and the Dean of Jersey, both militant and stubborn, refused to give up their bit of power. The Dean summoned the Bailiff, the King's Advocate and the Captain of the Castle, to appear before the Bishop. They were accused of, 'attacking the authority of the Church'. In the meanwhile, the Dean and his pack of clerics continued to sling people into the Bishop's prison for any crime they thought might be dealt with by the Church, from drunkenness or womanizing, to blasphemy or getting their fingers stuck in the poor-box. This was regardless of the new law, the Pope, the King, Otho or anyone.

This called for another Assizes, and the Justices duly arrived to sort things out. They arrested thirty-three people who had been 'causing the subjects of the King to be summoned out of the Realm'. They were dispatched to the French cooler by the Dean's clan. A Prior was fined for creating alarm and despondency in the camp by starting a rumour that the Justices themselves were to be arrested by armed men sent by the Bishop.

After this promising start, next day, whilst the Assizes was in full swing, the Dean and a large crowd of clerics descended on the Court like a flock of crows and began issuing demands and insisting that some clerics imprisoned in Guernsey should be released immediately, regardless of the charges against them. Arguments swayed back and forth, but the Dean refused to listen to any opinion except his own, or accept any authority except that of his beloved Bishop. He then proceeded to excommunicate everyone in sight, plus the entire population of Jersey if they failed to obey him. He was immediately arrested, but his clerics became violent and rescued him from prison. So, despite everything, the Church won the day, for, no sooner had the Justices left the Island, than that deadly duo, the Dean and the Bishop, carried on with business as usual, doing their own thing, deporting so called transgressors to the jail in Coutances.

It was an unfortunate fact of life, that whenever the Justices had reason to deal with the Islands, they lost no opportunity to grab all the cash that they could in the form of fines, presumably, for the King's piggy bank.

The lengths they would go to for this purpose would have been laughable had they not been so totally unjust. The whole of St Helier was fined because a robbery had not been reported. When a house in St Ouen was broken into, they couldn't find out who committed the crime so everyone in that Parish was fined. This went on until, eventually, the King recognized the injustice of Sir Otho's people being Justices in local cases and so put a stop to that.

Sir Otho and his Bailiffs still had a trick or two up their collective sleeve. Using a copy of the King's Seal, they made up laws as they went along, and, of course, these laws always involved someone paying out for something. If the person refused to hand over yet another handful of money, they would incarcerate him in the Castle, using the authority of the King's seal.

Once again, the King ordered an investigation. This time, however, some members of the Assizes really did have the interests of the Islands at heart and went for the throat when it came to corrupt officials. One such was hanged and another took off like a rat up a drainpipe before he suffered the same fate. Many others were fined. Several parcels of land were returned to their rightful owners, but then, after all that, Otho, the wily warden, whispered in the King's ear, and the Poltroon reversed that decision. The land was turned over to Otho and what was left of his rogues.

Now the Islanders were close to revolution, and when, in 1324, as a final straw, Sir Otho's nephew arrived in Guernsey as a Sub Warden, the local lads just slung him into prison. This act so bestirred Old Otho, that he left his castle in Switzerland and, at the age of nearly ninety, actually set foot in the Channel Islands for the first time. No one was impressed. Another petition and another set of Justices arrived. Included in their number was Henry Spigurnel, a fierce old Judge who had no favourites. Before The Assizes had even had a chance to sit down, let alone ask questions, Otho nipped off as fast as his aged legs would take him, back to his Swiss castle.

Judge Spigurnel then proceeded to set up what might be termed, a constitution of fair play. Its official title was 'The Ordinance for the Good of the Isle', and it instituted many changes:

* The Courts were to meet every one or two weeks.
* Any verdict decided upon by seven jurats was ironclad.
* There should be no time wasted in coming to decisions and giving verdicts.
* Advocates must swear not to prolong a case by making silly points and objections.
* Landowners must keep roads bordering their estates and fiefs in good repair.
* Anyone buying flour or corn was entitled to keep an eye on the measures.
* All weights had to be tested and sealed by the Bailiff and two Jurats.

To the great joy of the lucky forty-eight who got the job, the Judge also decided that there should be four beer tasters in each parish. The job description was that they should visit every tavern and sample every cask of beer, wine or cider three times, first when it was opened, next when half full and lastly when nearly empty. It is not thought that the tavern keepers ever tried to bribe the tasters with free drinks on the house.

1327 saw the end of an era of oppression and corruption, up to a point. Sir Otho died and Edward the Poltroon was disposed of. the Island's fifty years of struggle had drawn Jersey men together and taught them to be united against injustice and interference. Those who rule us must maintain the ancient customs of the Island.

Edward III felt that he had the right to be King of France, mainly because he was the nephew of King Philip. There was a lot of wrangling but, in the end, the job went to Philip of Valois who was the cousin of the old King and really was French.

Edward, though no doubt a bit miffed, did not let this deter him from waging war on the Scots for several years, a war which, amazingly, was to have dire effects on the Channel Islands in the future.

Considering the population of Jersey was only about twelve thousand, it is strange how much interest Parliament continued to take in their affairs. In 1331, more Judges and Justices arrived to challenge the ancient rights of the Islands. To their surprise, in Guernsey they were met with a strong force made up of men from both Jersey and Guernsey and, bizarrely, some Basque wine merchants and French Monks who loudly and bitterly pointed out that the King had no right to change the ways of the Channel Islands. They threatened mayhem and bloodshed if he tried to.

The Justices were having none of this. The assembled crowd backed up the protesters by shouting rude remarks about the King and making threats. They were arrested. They cunningly demanded their right of trial by jury. They got it and of course the jury, made up of local men, declared them all to be as innocent as babes and the case was dismissed. Feeling very put out, the Justices came over to Jersey where they declared a mistrial, but the matter just faded out. Determined not to be idle, the Justices decided to probe and question the customs and rights of the Islands yet again. Trying to show their authority, they even re-arrested a young cleric who had spent three years in the Coutances jail for accidentally killing the Lieutenant Bailiff. This unhappy lad had just been released by the Bishop and returned to the Island, when the Justices pounced. The Dean stepped on that one very quickly. The Justices were overruled and the young man was released once again.

In the meanwhile, Edward, who had been fighting with the Scots, had at last succeeded in knocking young David Bruce off the Scottish Throne. It was a calamity for the Islands. David Bruce escaped from the English troops and managed to get himself down to France. Intent upon revenge and with the help of King Philip, he gathered up a fleet of cut throats, sailed up the channel and vented his bad temper on Jersey and Guernsey. This mixture of Celts, kilts and garlic proved to be as blood thirsty and vicious a lot as any had yet seen. Murder, arson and every horror their evil minds could devise were perpetrated with comparative ease, as the Islands had no organized defence.

As it was definitely on the cards that this new enemy would soon be back to have another go at what they no doubt considered a 'soft' target, Edward 111 ordered the Warden, Thomas de Ferrers, to enlist every able bodied man to form a well armed defence force. This may have been the origin of the Militia. As well as the attacks on the Channel Islands, there were a lot of warlike actions and nasty little incidents. Eventually Edward got totally fed up with it all and declared war on France which was to last one hundred years.

In 1338, Admiral Béhuchet of France came with an immense army. Again the devastation was horrendous. The only thing they couldn't capture was The Castle, now Mont Orgueil. Despite a six month siege the flag of St George continued to flutter, so Admiral Béhuchet took himself off to the other islands and captured the lot. Two years later, he was to regret his bold actions.

The French King, disillusioned with trying to totally control Jersey, passed responsibility for the Islands over to his son Jean. Young Jean was not impressed and rapidly got rid of Robert Bertrand, Seigneur of Normandy, and Marshall of France. Jean whistled up an army of 8000 with some fifty ships and arrived in Jersey. First they decided that a parley would be favourite, so the defenders of The Castle met them in 'no man's land' but were not taken in by the promises of the wily French Marshall. Promises that the King of France would restore the Island's liberties and grant whatever franchises the Islanders wanted were recognized for what they were, a cunning ploy to turn the defenders against the English who, so far, had not granted them much in that line. The local lads remained loyal to the Crown and after suggesting that the French might care to go away, nipped back inside to man the barricades.

After a good look around, the French realized that The Castle was too well defended so, instead of attacking it, they just ran riot over the rest of the Island and, with their usual charm, they indulged in the routine pillage and burning before heading off home to Normandy. They returned twice that year and ignoring The Castle did their thing around the rest of the Island. They didn't quite get away scot free, as several stalwarts sneaked out from The Castle and did a commando raid on the invaders, killing nearly fifty of them.

Not all Jersey men were as loyal as others. Some high ranking individuals who had become disillusioned with the attitude of the English Government, actually threw in their lot with the invaders and assisted them whenever possible. When their duplicity came to light, a Jurat and a Seigneur had their property confiscated. These two quislings headed off for France rather quickly where they were welcomed and rewarded with land and property.

In 1340, Béhuchet, that Admiral of France who had celebrated the start of the hundred-year war by battering the Channel Islands, got his comeuppance. King Edward had now gained command of the sea and when the Admiral was captured, the King avenged the Islands by hanging him from his own masthead.

Edward was well pleased with 'the faithful and beloved men of the isles' for their bravery and loyalty, and at last granted them all the privileges, rights, immunities and honours that the Islanders knew were theirs anyway. That the King now knew it as well was felt to be a distinct advantage!

Unfortunately, tranquillity was not to reign long in the Channel Islands. In 1341, a new Warden, Sir Thomas of Hampton, had been appointed. He had actually bought the Wardenship. As no one pays out good money unless they expect to reap big rewards, you just had to hope that they intended to do it fairly and honestly. Unfortunately, both the new Warden and his Lieutenant, Henry de La More, were a right pair of scoundrels.

Henry had been done for embezzlement in England and only got off by wangling a pardon from the King. Having got a bit of power as Warden's toady, the true character of the fellow came out.

He became a high-handed tyrant and quickly destroyed the good will Edward had won in the Islands. Money and goods that the people had placed in The Castle for safe keeping during troubled times were quickly taken over by Henry de La More, and he was hanging on to them no matter what. The King ordered that these goods and chattels be returned to their owners, but that was only the tip of the iceberg.

It would seem that about this time a bit of a revolt had broken out against these dictators, as there were reports of many people being killed and houses burnt down. When the Warden brought in three hundred toughs, dredged from the sewers of Southampton and Portsmouth, a reign of intimidation, terror and murder followed.

Whilst King Edward was on a day trip to France, a boatload of Jersey men managed to flag him down. They explained the situation and their problems, however there seems to have been some suspicion or confusion on the King's part as he ended up thinking that the Islanders were in revolt against him and his officers. Luckily this breakdown in communication was resolved when the Commissioners who had been sent over by the King, realized that the villains of the piece were the wicked Warden and his lethal Lieutenant. These two miscreants were recalled but there seems to be no mention of punishment, or 'compo' for the Islanders.

1347 saw the arrival of the deadliest invader yet - The Black Death. This virulent plague, which spread from China, is thought to have dispatched about a third of the world's population to a better place. Normandy was ravaged and lost 100,000 souls. Jersey was not immune. Many of the clergy, including ten Rectors succumbed to the pestilence. No doubt because of this, written records of life and death around this period are scarce, but the fact that the King waived the fishing tax on the few surviving local fishermen speaks for itself.

The Black Death ultimately had an affect on communication. Ever since 1066, when the Normans and Jersey captured England, the language of polite society, the clergy and the law was French. This meant that Jersey could speak, or complain to Parliament in a common language, but after that lethal epidemic, so many people of rank had died, that more lowly persons and so called peasants, began to take their place in Church and Law. Soon, Jersey, who continued with Norman French, were speaking a different language. This confusion continued for many years until Jersey gradually became more anglicized. The Black Death had a devastating affect on France. This, and the internal strifes of that time, allowed Jersey a bit of a breather.

In 1356, somehow, despite all their troubles at home, the French went and captured Guernsey's Castle Cornet. This united the Islands against a common foe. The Bailiff of Jersey, a handful of Seigneurs plus a sizeable force of fierce locals nipped over for a punch-up with the invaders. During the fierce hand to hand fighting, they managed to capture the Captain of the French forces. He immediately offered the Jersey Commanders 80,000 French florins for his release. In a rare burst of honesty for those days, they refused his money and released the Captain free of charge provided that he surrendered the castle. The alliance between Jersey and Guernsey was short lived. The Common Council of armed men, a sort of lower ranks assembly had caught and executed a traitor. Unfortunately, the traitor was a Guernsey man and this was unforgivable. The Guernsey court ordered the arrest of the Jersey men responsible. Although neither of the Seigneurs, de Carteret and Lempriere, had been involved in any way, they stood by their lads and assumed responsibility for the execution. These honourable men were found guilty by the Guernsey court and imprisoned in a dungeon. For two years, legal arguments and ploys raged. The widow of the dead traitor was to the fore in stirring things up, but despite that, in the end, the two unhappy Seigneurs obtained the King's pardon, mainly because of their gallant efforts in the freeing of Castle Cornet for the ungrateful Guernsey people.

In 1360, a treaty was signed between England and France. A clause in that useful document was that the French would keep their hands off the Channel Islands. It was a few years grace to give the Islanders time to rebuild and thatch their cottages in readiness for the next bonfire.

An odd incident about that time indicated the domestic savagery of the age. A chap called Jehannet was unwise enough to suggest that the wife of the owner of Rozel Manor was an adulteress. She was really miffed about this. She said that slanderers should have their tongues torn out and she told her two sons to go and sort him out. They set an ambush, jumped him and tore out his tongue. The two young thugs then fled to Normandy. One of them disappeared but the other was arrested and hanged. The father was so fed up that he sold the manor and left for England.

In 1373, our brief years of peace and tranquillity come to an abrupt end at the hands of a Welshman! His name was Owen. This son of Wales was very displeased with King Edward because he had killed his father who was a minor Welsh prince. Owen went to France and, with the help of the French King, he got an army of 600 soldiers together. He intended to take them to Wales and start a revolt. He was very full of himself and full of threats and boasts about how he would recover the throne of his ancestors. In a blaze of rhetoric and bombast, he set sail for Wales with his brave army. On reaching Guernsey it seems that he couldn't wait to get to Wales so he started revolting there instead.

The usual killing, burning and destruction were the order of the day throughout the Island. They then slipped over to Jersey for more of the same. By this time Owen had obviously forgotten about the land-of-his-father and decided that it would be more fun to lay siege to Castle Cornet in Guernsey but the French King wanted his soldiers back, so he ordered Owen to pack it in and come home.

The Channel Islanders were not happy but King Edward promised to keep an eye on things and to have a few ships ready to sail to the Islands' assistance if another mob with sharp swords and a box of matches turned up.

The Black Dog of Brittany, Bertrand du Guesclin was a Breton Squire. He was also a brilliant military tactician. For five years he had been giving the British a real lesson in the art of battle and siege. It was in 1373, when he had Brest under siege, that the British Commander agreed to surrender if no help arrived within a month. Bertrand was contemplating a few quiet weeks when one of his Captains with a big mouth said, 'how about having a bash at Jersey whilst we are waiting'. Bertrand, who was starting to get bored anyway, jumped at the idea. It was October when the Black Dog with 2,000 soldiers and 600 bowmen were knocking on the door of Gorey Castle.

The only answer they got was rocks and arrows flying from every loophole. Try as they may, the French could not get a foot in the door and many died trying. Not to be defeated, the wily Commander set his sappers to dig under the outer wall, not an easy task when people keep dropping stones on your head! However with the aid of mattocks and picks, they succeeded in digging away until a section of wall came crashing down. Fearing that the end was nigh, the Bailiff insisted that the castle Commander should negotiate to surrender. Terms were agreed, including payment of a ransom and a promise that the Islanders would become loyal subjects of the French King. Little did the defenders realize that the French scaling ladders were too short to be of much use, or that the sappers were finding the Jersey granite walls and foundations exceptionally hard. They couldn't have known either that Bertrand had that siege in Brest to finish off and didn't want to hang around too long anyway.

Had all this been known to them, they surely would have continued their brave defence. They didn't know, they surrendered, and the British Government, with the wisdom of hindsight, blamed the Bailiff and clapped him in the Tower of London charged with treason. Luckily, the council that was set up to deal with the case soon realized that he was not guilty. He was released and given his old job back.

The Castle, meanwhile, was back in British hands, but The Black Dog's people were still taking liberties with the rest of Jersey and forcing the payments of more ransoms by imprisoning and burning to death any who would not agree to pay.

In the end, even the French realized, after words of advice from both the Pope and King Edward, that they were trying to flog the blood out of a dead stone horse. Jersey had been 'hit' so many times that there simply was nothing left.

King Edward III of England and the King of France died within three years of each other, no doubt intent on continuing the battle elsewhere. By coincidence, 1380 then saw both countries in the tender hands of eleven-year-old children. Both children were lumbered with totally incompetent uncles who acted, or attempted to act, as Regents. The poor leadership allowed the on-going war to languish through lack of interest, but naturally unpleasantness and raids continued on both sides.

Jersey was a bit entangled in the middle of all this, so France who were at this time being big chums with Castile, decided that as the Channel Islands were being used as a base for raids on Brittany, it would be best if everyone was shipped out, every house burned to the ground and even every tree chopped down. This became known in modern times as the 'scorched earth' policy.

Jean de Vienne, a very famous French Admiral was sent over to do the business and destroy the isles. For some reason he decided not to carry out his instructions. There were good guys around even in those desperate times!

It is interesting to note that in 1306, the Bailiff of St Martin, who had been accused of treason and then given his old job back, was re-arrested for treason by the new Warden, Sir Hugh de Calvely. Despite his wife's efforts to plead his cause, he was locked up in Gorey Castle for four years. It was only by escaping from his cell, bending King Richard's ear and throwing himself on his mercy, that he got a retrial. This ill-used chap was again found not guilty and released, but this time he didn't get his old job back.

For a while, no one was officially banging away at Jersey, so when in 1378, Pope Gregory X1 followed the French King to the promised land, this left scope for ecclesiastical infighting and confrontation in a big way involving Popes, Bishops, Rectors and Deans in Rome, France, England and of course Jersey. At one point, this led to one lot leading a crusade in a bungled attempt to wipe out a rival faction in Europe, in a very Christian manner of course!

Whilst this was going on, the English Parliament was in full and merciless flood, executing the King's friends and generally being cold-blooded and bloody-minded in the pursuit of power. It was eleven years before Richard 11 was in a position to take revenge but when he did, he came down on those parliamentary leaders like a ton of rocks. Revenge was sweet and many of those evil men were condemned to death, including eighty-year-old Sir John Cobham who was sentenced to be hung, drawn and quartered! However, in the end, because of his age, they probably thought the shock would be too much for him and he was condemned to spend what was left of his life in Gorey castle.

By now King Richard was eager for peace with France. Perhaps the word desperate might be more appropriate, as he agreed to marry Isabella, the scrawny seven-year-old daughter of Charles V11 of France. Once Richard was 'family,' his father-in-law reckoned he was on to a good thing. He began by demanding the return of various bits of France that were in English possession, Richard agreed. Then Charles went for the jugular. He demanded that the Channel Islands be surrendered to France, as they were, he decided, part of Normandy. Once again, Lady Luck was with the Islands as, before Richard could make the decision to hand them over, he was taken prisoner in Wales and carried off to London.

His conduct as he grew older had given much cause for concern. His tyrannical behaviour had led his subjects to believe that no one was safe from this poor unbalanced soul.

Arriving in London, he was taken to the Tower and forced to sign his abdication and confirm that he was insufficient and useless. He was never seen again, except by his gaolers. One good thing was that poor old Sir John Cobham was released from Gorey Castle. His cell door swung open as Richard's closed.

CHAPTER FOUR
1400 - 1500

Jersey's privileges were confirmed once again by the new man, King Henry 1V. In 1400, he also decided to have a knock at the Bishop of Coutances, referring to him as 'that son of treason' and withdrawing his jurisdiction.

The crown did not sit easily on Henry's head as he was seen as a usurper. There were rumours doing the rounds that Richard had escaped from the Tower and was intent on grabbing back the throne just as Henry was about to sit down. Even Jersey men were said to be involved in the plot. In fact, there was no real danger, just a few hot heads with nothing better to do. No one wanted to see poor deranged Richard back and poking his nose into their affairs, but Henry did get worried and told the Warden of Jersey to put down the 'revolt'!

It was July 1403 and Jersey was under attack again. Although there was still a truce between England and France, a small fleet of English freebooters (privateers out after free booty) attacked and plundered merchant ships around the Brittany coast. Admiral Jean de Penhouet of Brittany decided to put a stop to this little escapade and took off in pursuit. There was a battle and the gallant Admiral defeated and took forty of the vessels as prizes. Flushed with success and excited, he looked around for another target - Jersey! Despite the truce, they burned houses, took prisoners, filched anything that wasn't nailed down and held the Island to ransom for huge amounts of money. The fact that Jersey was an innocent party was not considered important to these boorish Bretons who were worse than the privateers they had defeated.

In 1406, whilst France and the Spaniards of Castile were still bosom friends, a Castilian, name of Pero Nino was prowling down the English Channel to see what he could find to plunder, when he met up with a group of French ships out on the same mission. As they were allies, they stopped for a chat. They soon told Nino about a fertile English island close by where fine pickings could be found - the Island of Jersey.

Pero Nino sailed to Harfleur, a haven of pirates and unsavoury characters. Here he met up with a Breton Knight who was a sort of floating, freelance scallywag. They agreed that an attack on Jersey would be worthwhile. At the time, the gallant Knight was only involved in escorting a small convoy of salt boats so he willingly consented to help. To beef up their large force of seamen, they enlisted a thousand men-at-arms in St Malo and, on October 7th, the Armada, including the salt boats, set sail. The following dawn saw Nino's army lined up on what is now West Park beach. Under the cover of linked shields, they advanced towards the shoreline watched by three thousand grim faced Jersey men. A sudden cavalry charge was almost decimated by a tremendous volley of arrows from the invaders. Another attack by the local men led to fierce hand to hand fighting. Boots, fists, daggers and swords were used on both sides to destroy the enemy. Limbs were hacked off, heads rolled and the blood flowed in torrents. The Jersey flag was captured in a final fierce melee, but by this time, both sides had fought one another to a standstill and were forced to back off and lick their wounds.

In the rather strange way that battles seem to have been fought in those times, the next day saw Nino and co. marching, presumably un-hindered, to what was described as a villa, where they had been told the loot would be found. This was a large enclosed area surrounded by a moat and barricades. It was capable of sheltering thousands of women, children and cattle, and of course a sizeable army of defenders. It is thought that this 'villa' may have been what is now known as Chastel Sedement at Trinity, part of which goes back to Roman times. Before attacking the villa, brave Nino had his men set fire to everything they could find in the area. Cottages, houses, crops and gardens were all put to the torch.

An approach was made to the Spanish captain for mercy. It was mentioned that the Queen of Castile was English but he was a hard-nosed mongrel and began berating the negotiators for assisting the English. He demanded all sorts of life long allegiances to just about everyone, including Castile, Spain, France and the ship's cat, or he would burn down the villa and slaughter everyone. Whilst he was doing his early impression of Hitler, several of the Captains had been having a snoop around. They realized that the villa was very well defended and the butcher's bill would be huge if they tried to capture it, especially against such sturdy foes as the Jersey men. When they could get a word in, they told Nino to cool it and explained the facts of life. He immediately lowered his sights. Everyone then settled for a ransom of 10,000 gold crowns, the release of French prisoners and, strangely, an annual tribute of a dozen each of axes, lances, bows and trumpets. Four important hostages were taken until all the gold had been paid over, later they were released. Meanwhile, whilst all this had been going on, the French sailors from the salt boats had come ashore and looted anything they could lay their thieving hands on and cleared off before they could be caught.

Things calmed down after that. The King of France went mad. The King of England, not to be outdone, contracted a rather nasty disease thought to be leprosy.

In 1412, young Henry V came, full of vim, vigour and ambition. His cures for the internal problems of his country have a parallel in today's politics. Keep the people's minds' busy with 'foreign quarrels'. France was to be his target. He decided first to clamp down on revenue from alien priories leaving the Island for France. This was his first move in placing the cat firmly in La Colomberie - (the pigeon loft.) Plan 'B' was to come later! Henry V spent the next couple of years aggravating the Island's clergy and ordered the tithe to be paid to the English treasury. Until now, this sizeable amount of loot had disappeared into the abbey's coffers in Normandy.

Next, Henry got Parliament to pass a law ordering all property owned by foreign ecclesiastics to be handed over to the Crown.

In 1415, the young King, who had married a French Princess, renewed his claim on France and backed it up with axe, arrow and fire. The capture of Harfleur, where pirates tended to forgather, was his first victory in what was to be a long and bloody campaign. He defeated the French army in the battle of Agincourt and conquered most of Normandy. Every boat in Jersey was called upon to help in the siege of Cherbourg and by 1419 all Normandy, with the exception of Mont Saint Michel, was an English province.

King Henry was well pleased and entered Paris at the head of his army in 1420. Many Jersey men were rewarded for their part in the fighting, but the biggest reward was that Jersey was now well within the English province and was safe from the French.

It was agreed that the English longbows were the deciding factor at Agincourt and were the ultimate weapon of the time. All agreed except for one English soldier. He was the first man to be killed by a bullet fired by the first experimental gun.

The great ecclesiastical rift had been cobbled together by persuading rival Popes to hang up their dogmas and step down. Pope Benedict X111 was now the new boss. All was peace and light in Jersey and the Bishop of Coutances was given his ball back.

In times of peace, trade and travel become firm favourites. Many people set off on pilgrimages to the shrine of St James in Northern Spain, but there were certain travel restrictions. You would not be allowed to take more gold or silver out of the country than was needed for 'personal use', also you must swear not to reveal any English secrets to those foreign persons. The Spanish 'resort' became very popular with local people - not unlike today, but without the restrictions.

Just like in the words of the song 'summertime and the living is easy', it was summertime for Jersey after all the trials, tribulations and terror of the recent conflicts. There was trade in corn, fish and butter with visiting ships and with foreign ports, but as the French navy was still about, traders needed to buy a 'safe conduct' from the Admirals. Both sides were into this little racket but they always honoured their permits to travel and safety was assured. There was also a good trade in all sorts of goodies brought into the Island by Jersey men who had 'liberated' them whilst fighting in France
.

A great deal of the new wealth was spent on enlarging and improving the churches. Although it seemed that lightning raids were a thing of the past, the Churches were roofed with barrel vaults of rubble stone as a precaution against raiders with flaming torches.

Gorey Castle.

Building and alteration were also being carried out at Gorey Castle. It was around 1460 that it got it's new name, Mont Orgueil (pronounced Mont Orgay). The King's brother, The Duke of Clarence, named Mount Pride. No doubt the many poor souls who had been incarcerated in its dank dungeons had a different name for it!

The old French King and the comparatively young Henry V, both died in 1422 and Henry V1 was proclaimed King of England and France. Just one snag, Henry was a baby. His Uncle, the Duke of Bedford had to carry the can for the next thirteen years! Luckily, the Duke was a capable and honourable man, but the situation he was trying to cope with was a formidable one.

The people of Southern France were still loyal to the old King's son, Charles. Meanwhile, in the occupied North, the English were deeply resented. As has happened since, the peasants of Northern France formed a resistance movement. Guerrilla attacks on English forces were frequent. In 1429 bad news came for England but, strangely, it was good news with mixed blessings, for the Channel Islands.

If things had remained as they were, Jersey today might well have been French. Henry V had dreamed of England and France becoming one united Kingdom. As France was the larger and wealthier country of the two, it is thought that almost certainly she would have eventually become the senior partner. No doubt the English court would have moved from Westminster to Paris and the overall lifestyle would have taken on a garlic aroma, whilst England would have been relegated to the status of an off shore province. The Channel Islands, being closest to the French coast would certainly have become French.

Jeanne d'Arc was only seventeen when she donned her white suit of armour and led the French army in revolt against the English. There was no man who would not follow her. She inspired such loyalty, that even after the English had captured and burned her at the stake, their excuse being that she must be a witch, the French troops fought on in her name. By 1450, the only bit of France still in English hands was Calais, and France had command of the sea.

When a new Warden, John Nanfan, was appointed to Jersey, he had to pay 250 Crowns to the French Admiral for safe passage across the Channel.

This is where the Islands enjoyed mixed blessings. They were definitely English, but were again prone to attack by the French. It was not long before Jersey was overrun and hostages were taken. The new Warden kindly paid 1000 of his own money for the Jersey hostages to be released from Cherbourg where their lives were at stake.

It was only two years after the last bitter war with France that the 'Wars of the Roses' began in 1455. This exceedingly messy civil war lasted thirty years with more treachery, coat turning and treason than you could shake a longbow at. Despite Yorkshire and Lancashire being quite a long way away, this domestic punch-up had a vital effect on Jersey for several years.

Very often sides were taken locally, but usually this was a case of bloody-mindedness during some petty feud with a neighbour. If a neighbour said he agreed with one side, his adversary would pledge undying support for the opposition. There were, however, some serious political disputes.

Both sides trusted the Warden, Nanfan, who was a good honest soldier, and he had the Island's welfare at heart. Unfortunately, because of commitments in the UK, he sometimes had to leave his deputy, Otys Colin, in charge for long periods.

Otys Colin was a very different cup of tea to the Warden. He was an ardent Yorkist and very opposed to the powerful de St Martin family who happened to be Lancastrians. In 1456, one of the de St Martin lads was wounded in the leg by some of Oyts Collin's men. The lad's mother complained about this, so Oyts had three more of her sons imprisoned in the Castle. The mother complained again, this time to the Courts. She appealed for their release. Oyts was ordered to bring the lads before the Court if he did indeed have any charge against them.

Instead of complying, cunning Oyts Colin had them sent off to Castle Cornet in Guernsey, which was out of the Jersey Court's jurisdiction. For two years they suffered the loathsome conditions of imprisonment in a dungeon with very little food. During a brief peace between the battling rose wearer's, the brothers were released and returned to Jersey. Of course the war did break out again and the Earl of Warwick, an ardent Yorkist, lost his control over the Channel Islands. The de St Martins once more gained positions of power in the Island, Guillaume becoming Attorney General.

French born Queen Marguerite, wife of Henry V1, was a strongly minded lady. She was very pro the Lancastrians cause and was related to Comte de Maulevrier who, in turn, was a cousin of one Jean Carbonnel.

On a dark night in 1461, Jean Carbonnel led a surprise attack by French forces on Mont Orgueil. It was hardly an attack, and not a surprise to some. It is thought that the wily Queen had set up the whole thing. When the French arrived, the door was open and the guards were drunk.

Marguerite presumably wanted the castle as a bolthole for herself and her husband, Henry, in case things became a bit thorny in the roses war. Guillaume de St Martin, who had been imprisoned and starved, had no love for the Yorkists and it was reckoned that he conspired with the Queen to let her relatives take over the castle. Whilst one can feel sympathy for the chap, it did mean that Jersey was to be under French occupation for the next seven years. Though some blamed Warden Nanfan for this, most branded Guillaume the traitor.

Comet de Maulevrier was determined to make the locals appreciate their new masters and granted many concessions in a charter known as 'The Ordinances of Maulevrier'. Under this, Jersey governed themselves, with the Bailiff, Jurats, Rectors and Constables in Assembly. This was probably the forerunner of the present States of Jersey.

The seven-year occupation seems, on the whole, to have been fairly painless. The Lady of St Ouen dined with the French Commander and his wife. When John Hareford, one of Warrick's men, landed at St Ouen, de Carteret promptly handed him over to the French. In the light of future events this may just have been a 'lulling suspicions' ploy.

The Bailiff, Nicolas Morin continued in office. Every time he signed a document, he was forced to sign as 'Bailiff, Under the High and Mighty Lord, The Count of Maulevrier, Lord of the Isles'.

How the 'High and Mighty' can fall, was demonstrated to the Count quite quickly. Charles VII of France died and his son Louis XI, took over. Because he had hated his father and logic wasn't his strong point, young Louis decided to get rid of all the old King's ministers.

Louis then changed his mind. He wanted the civil war in England to keep going. As the Lancastrians weren't doing too well, he offered the Count a deal. Provided Maulevrier was willing to take a small army across the channel and give them, and Queen Marguerite, a hand, he would be a free man. Naturally the Count agreed and in 1462 he headed for Northumbria with Queen Margie.

Jean Carbonnel, who led the raid on Mont Orgueil, had a cousin by the name of Guillaume and this young man was put in charge of the Island whilst Jean was doing a spot of pillage up in the North of England. Guillaume seemed to think that some skulduggery was afoot. He felt sure that someone was out to capture the Castle so he devised a cunning plan involving an English prisoner.

The Englishman, John Hareford, had been part of a foraging party that landed at St Ouen. He was the only one to be caught and became a resident at Mont Orgueil.

John was a personable young man and was obviously well educated. He also knew which side his bread was buttered and was ready to please. Guillaume suggested that he might allow the prisoner parole to mix with the pro English gentry and their wives. He also suggested that John should report back to him any loose talk or revolutionary mutterings he might overhear.

Young Hareford mixed freely with his new friends by fishing, helping with the harvest dining and playing 'Fives', which was a sort of ancestor of squash. In a comparatively short time he picked up enough information for arrests to be made.

Renaud Lempriere, The Seigneur of Rozel and Thomas Le Hardy, the elderly Rector of St Martin, were put on trial. Whether there really was a plot at that time is difficult to say. The mound of evidence dredged up, mainly by John Hareford, sounded almost too much and too good to be true.

He said that the old Rector had asked him during confession if he would help drive out the French. He told the Court that the Seigneur had offered him one hundred Crowns to leave a door open at the Castle. He also said he had been shown a letter from Guernsey offering sixty men to help attack and capture Mont Orgueil. Sixty good Guernsey men risking life and limb to free a Jersey castle was not believable.

The prisoners and Lempriere's wife, Katherine, were cross-examined very thoroughly for nearly two days but totally denied the whole thing. The French really did not want trouble in the Island so, despite some suspicion, they decided the matter was really not all that important. Eventually the prisoners were pardoned and released. It would seem that justice was done, as neither of these men nor their families were exactly firebrands.

Renaud Lempriere was forty-five. His wife Katherine was twenty-two and they had two young children. His fifteen-year-old niece lived with them and helped around the house. Also living with them was Renaud's illegitimate son, Jean. With the sensitivity shown to such matters in those days, the teenager was known as the 'Bastard of Rozel'. They held Mass every morning in their private Chapel and attended Church twice on Sundays. Perhaps Renaud was trying to atone for having fathered an illegitimate child. He certainly thought nothing of thrashing the lad on any flimsy excuse. Despite that the Seigneur was a homebody, hospitable and very proud of his gardens.

The other suspected revolutionary, Thomas Le Hardy, the elderly Rector of St Martin, spent most of his time riding his mule around the parish saying Mass anywhere and everywhere. He led a quiet life with two men servants and with his young cousin, who acted as his Curate. He was as hospitable as he could afford to be and liked to share a mazer (wooden drinking bowl) of beer with friends after the service.

When Jean Carbonnel arrived back in the Island after his depredations in Northern England, things had changed. France was having a civil war. Maulevrier had been killed. Normandy, which had achieved independence with it's own Duke, which would have pleased Jean, had been recaptured by the French King, Louis XI. Louis knew Jean supported the Duke of Normandy so Jean Carbonnel was in trouble with both his own King plus the King of England. On top of this, his position had weakened. The Islanders began to show their true unfriendly feelings. Jean retired promptly to Mont Orgueil.

The Castle was well fortified and his friend The Duke had sent over a large supply of gunpowder.

Philippe de Carteret, Seigneur of St Ouen, was not a friend of the French, despite wining and dining them occasionally. When some of his activities started to ring alarm bells with M. Carbonnel in his Castle, the order went out that the Seigneur was to be arrested.

Philippe was quietly fishing in a pond a couple of miles from the Manor when, out of the corner of his eye, he spotted a party of French soldiers creeping silently towards him intent, he suspected, on doing him no good. Dropping his fishing line, he leapt on to his horse and headed for home across the fields. Suddenly a troop of French horsemen appeared, cutting off his retreat. There was only one escape route and this was across a sunken lane. The lane was eighteen feet deep and twenty-two feet wide but the Seigneur had no choice. At full gallop he set his horse at the gap. With a mighty leap the gallant animal cleared it. Landing safely on the other side, they galloped on across Les Landes leaving their pursuers far behind. As they reached the gates of the Manor, the horse stumbled and dropped dead beneath him. He was so proud of the animal and so upset at its death that the Seigneur had his old friend buried in his garden at St Ouen's Manor. The three hundred year old bones were rediscovered not long ago.

In 1468, Vice Admiral Richard Harliston sailed a few of his ships to Guernsey. Leaving them at anchor, he took a small boat over to Jersey and landed secretly at Plémont. The night was black as he made his way across the country to St Ouen's Manor for a meeting with Philippe de Carteret. They spent some time in conference and a plan was laid. A quick handshake and the Vice Admiral slipped away in to the night.

It was pitch dark as the Vice Admiral approached Jersey but this time he was aboard his ship and accompanied by his flotilla. Troops were landed and marched to St Ouen's Manor where de Carteret was waiting with as many 'resistance fighters' as he could raise. Together they marched along the north coast heading for Mont Orgueil Castle.

When Jean Carbonnel threw back the curtains next morning, the Castle was completely surrounded, on land by English troops and local men, whilst at sea; Vice Admiral Harliston's ships completed the blockade.

As provisions began to run short, Carbonnel decided to have a boat built which could slip out and fetch supplies. Knowing that the besiegers would hear the hammering and guess what he was up to, he cunningly had a dummy boat built in full view. Naturally the real boat would be all ready for use whilst the Trojan was still being hammered and fussed over.

The ploy might have worked but for one true Jersey man who was being forced to work inside the Castle. Once he realized what was afoot, he crept up on to the battlements in the dead of night and fired an arrow with a message attached into his allies' lines. A few nights later when the French went to launch their boat, English soldiers, lying in wait, surprised and captured them.

Meanwhile, the Duke of Normandy, not wishing to let his friend Jean down, and intent on retaining the only castle he had left, sent a boat from St Malo. The 'Jehanette' loaded with reinforcements, plus delicious fares like biscuits, dried cod, cider and a few casks of dragon's blood, which was a resinous powder, used as medicine and plasters, managed to slip through the blockade and unload at the Castle. These goodies allowed the Frenchman to hold out for another two months. However, after a total of nineteen weeks under siege, he decided that enough was enough and waved the white flag.

He was allowed to march out with full honours. Sir Richard the Vice Admiral and Philippe de Carteret, Seigneur of St Ouen, then marched in. The King's banners soon flew from every tower. The occupation was over and the gallant mariner became Jersey's Governor. Before anyone could draw breath, the English Civil war was back on again and a totally confused situation ensued.

People changed sides and roses. Alliances were forged, and then broken. Kings were on and off the Throne in a demented game of musical chairs. A local Seigneur and landowner then decided to put his four-pence worth in. Rounding up most of his tenants, he set off by ship to fight someone, anyone, with the wrong coloured rose.

As it happened, he seemed to have had a go at the wrong side. He was killed and the surviving Jersey lads decided it was time to go home. It wasn't their fight anyway. Reaching Southampton, they tried their luck at getting a boat to the island but their luck was out. They were captured and, though a few escaped, most of them were hanged as traitors.

It was not always doom, gloom and more doom. Two gratifying events did actually take place. First, in 1477, The Rector of St Saviour, Jean Hue, offered a field to the Island on which a school could be built. His kind offer was eventually accepted and a Grammar school was built. It mainly taught Latin grammar from 6am to 6pm every day. In 1480, the English King Edward IV died, and the French King Louis XI agreed after some nudging from the Pope, that in the event of war, the Channel Islands should be considered neutral. This happy state lasted just over two hundred year. In 1689, William III cancelled the deal. Around 250 years later, in 1940, Adolf Hitler ignored it as well!

In 1483 King Edward IV was dead. His little son was King of England. Ten weeks later he was dead, murdered. Who did it, or why, is in doubt but it left the way open for his uncle to don the crown as King Richard III. Meanwhile, over in Brittany, Henry Tudor, Earl of Richmond was encouraged by the Lancastrian Red Rose party to go for the English throne. On his way across the channel, a tremendous storm blew up and scattered his fleet. Henry Tudor ended up in Jersey with a red face. A chap called Clement Le Hardy arrived. Clement gave Henry food and shelter and later he helped him to get back to Normandy.

In 1485, presumably the weather forecast was favourable, so Henry Tudor set off once more to invade England and grab the crown. King Richard III was killed in battle so, Henry VII succeeded. He was the fourth King in two years. One of his first acts as King was to reward Clement Le Hardy by making him Bailiff of Jersey.

Sir Richard Harliston, that brave Vice Admiral, had governed Jersey successfully for fifteen years, but politics, those Roses again, got in the way. He wanted to involve Jersey in the Yorkist cause. The local Seigneurs didn't want to know. Word got to King Henry. Sir Richard, who had now lost all support in the Island, had to take refuge in Mont Orgueil.

He was eventually pardoned but now Jersey had a new Governor. Two new Governors, Matthew Baker and David Philippe, were both old friends of the King. David Philippe later became Governor of Guernsey but he doesn't appear to have had much interest in either Island as he spent most of his time in England seeking advancement.

Governor Matthew Baker was the main-man. He was also a high handed, malicious and vindictive man. He exasperated the Seigneurs by continuously questioning their rights and demanding to see their title deeds. He doubled the rents of tenants of Crown land and was just generally obnoxious.

Naturally there was a flood of protests to the Privy Council. Seigneur Philippe De Carteret as a Jurat acted as spokesman for the Island. For that reason, Matthew Baker set out to destroy him.

First he forged a letter, supposedly coming from De Carteret, to some noblemen in Normandy offering to betray Mont Orgueil to the French. The letter was dropped in a lane where Baker 'found' it whilst riding with his henchmen. He ordered one of them to read it out aloud, then immediately set off for town.

Full of feigned righteous indignation, he burst into the Court where Philippe De Carteret was acting as Jurat. Straight off he began shouting the odds and waving the letter and his fists at poor Philippe. Of course the flabbergasted chap denied it. Baker then played a cunning stroke. He challenged De Carteret to ordeal by battle. This was a virtually obsolete method of settling a matter. The idea was that The Good Lord would be on the side of truth and would therefore smite the ungodly and smile upon the virtuous, making sure he won. The church had abolished this form of trial a couple of hundred years back but, it was still on the statute-book and therefore, technically, legal. At this point, one of Bakers cohorts', a great bully of a man named Le Boutillier, threw down his gauntlet and demanded to do battle with De Carteret, thus allowing God to prove him a traitor.

Philippe De Carteret was Seigneur of St Ouen. He was a Jurat and a gentleman. He protested that Le Boutillier was a criminal whom he had, at one time, saved from the gallows. He said that it was not right that he should be expected to fight such a fellow. That should have been an end to the challenge but politics came to the fore. Clement Le Hardy who was made Bailiff for assisting 'Red Rose' King Henry - allowed the ordeal to go ahead.   He also refused bail. Both men were sent to Mont Orgueil until August 10th.

Le Boutillier was treated well, allowed exercise, and given as much to eat as he wished. Meanwhile, incarcerated in a dark, dank cell, De Carteret grew weaker on a diet of bread and water.

As if this was not bad enough, hidden trenches were dug in the grounds with the intention of tripping De Carteret during the fight. Presumably Le Boutillier would be warned of these traps in advance.

On top of all this, Baker tried to make sure that none of poor Philippe's friends could appeal to the King on his behalf. He ordered that no boats could leave Jersey. Just in case, he set off for England to put his false, one sided story to his friend, King Henry. At this point one could say that the odds were well and truly stacked against Philippe De Carteret.

A most remarkable woman, Margaret De Carteret entered into the fray. Her father was ex Governor Harliston and, during her marriage to Philippe, it was believed she bore twenty sons and a daughter. Despite having had a baby only three days before her husband's arrest, as soon as she heard of his plight, she was up and taking action. She knew that her only hope lay in getting to the King before Baker. She persuaded a fisherman to row her over to Guernsey. Here she contacted a Jurat de Beauvoir whose mother was from St Ouen in Jersey. He immediately agreed to sail her over to England. As they entered Poole harbour, they spotted Baker up ahead but, whilst he was sheltering from a sudden hailstorm, Margaret slipped ashore and headed off for Sheen where the King was staying.

Luck was with her and she was able to get hold of Bishop Fox of Durham who took her straight to King Henry. The King listened carefully to her story. Margaret was so eloquent that he signed an order forthwith forbidding the trial by combat. The case was to be heard in the proper way by the council. As Margaret came happily down the Palace steps, she met a belated and extremely miffed Matthew Baker hurrying up them.

Even now the race was not yet won. The combat was due to take place in just a few days time, so Margaret needed to get home fast. Luckily, again, she found a boat in Southampton due to set sail for Jersey. Margaret arrived on the Island just one day before the fight was due to take place. The King's order had to be obeyed. The contest was cancelled. Margaret had saved her husband's life. At the subsequent trial by council, his name was cleared and Baker lost his job as Governor of Jersey.

It would seem that 'trial by ordeal' actually had taken place between Margaret and Matthew Baker. Margaret De Carteret had won hands down.

A strange twist ended this tale. When barrels of wine from a Spanish wreck washed up on the beach at St Ouen, the Seigneurs of those Fiefs were well pleased and filled their wine cellars. Clement Le Hardy, as Bailiff, was supposed to take care of a certain portion for the King. Being greedy, he decided to grab most of it for his own cellar. Matthew Baker, whom Le Hardy had backed over the trial by combat issue, found out about his little wine lake. His last act before ceasing to be Governor was to throw Le Hardy into a dungeon. Clement Le Hardy eventually died there in the most appalling conditions.

Very soon after this, the powers of future Governors were curtailed by order of the King and Council.

Rozel Harbour.

St Ouen's Manor.

CHAPTER FIVE
1500 - 1600

Now, for the first time, Jersey was given a Governor who was a very amenable and helpful chap.

Thomas Overy was a merchant who had been Mayor of Southampton. He knew about trade and used his knowledge to the advantage of the Island for some years.

As Jersey was no longer part of Normandy, having a Bishop in Coutances was considered a no-no. King Henry was able to persuade the Pope, Alexander Borgia to issue a Bill transferring the Islands from the jurisdiction of Coutances to that of Salisbury. Three years later, in 1499, this was transferred to Winchester. Jersey was much closer to Coutances than Winchester, so the French Bishops continued to act in Jersey for fifty years exactly as they always had.

Anyone who got a scholarship to go to Victoria College can feel gratitude to Jean Neal. He was a Jersey man who became master at Arundel College. With the aid of a friend, Vincent Tehy, another Jersey man, Mayor of Southampton, Neal founded two grammar schools in St Peter. They were to last over three hundred years. Now their endowments are used to get likely lads those scholarships.

Thomas Lempriere, the Bailiff, owned a house in Morier Lane. It was stuffed with registers, records and documents relating to Jersey. This house burnt down and to the horror of future historians, all the paperwork went up in smoke.

Having a fine man like Thomas Overy as Governor was too good to last. When he died, Captain Sir Hugh Vaughan from Wales replaced him. He was a handsome fellow, gallant and courteous when it suited. He was a fine horseman. He was also a bully and a rapist with no respect for the law, people or property. Young girls could not walk the lanes for fear of being raped. Two men whose property the good Captain coveted, were beaten so severely that they died. He imprisoned a Chaplain until he handed over a letter, which allowed him to lay claim to an endowment of weekly Mass. He stole the takings. If Sir Hugh wanted a property he altered the deeds in his favour. His answer to any complaint was the sword.

By 1513, things got so bad that the Bailiff, Thomas Lempriere travelled to Westminster and made a complaint. Ignoring the new ruling that only the King could replace a Bailiff, he sacked Lempriere and installed Helier de Carteret, a son of the St Ouen Seigneur,as Bailiff. He was banking on young Henry VII being too absorbed in his pleasures to notice. He was right, but the Council did notice! In 1515, they sent over a Commission to investigate, but the St Ouen's Seigneur, the new Bailiff's dad, got it hushed up. Vaughan had won, but then he made a mistake. He fell out with the de Carteret's Stupidly, he tried to grab Trinity Manor for himself. This was, of course, illegal and it went to Court.

When Vaughan saw that judgement was going against him, he threatened to 'thrust his sword through the Bailiff's belly'. The Bailiff, young de Carteret, grabbed Vaughan, telling him that if he moved he was a dead man. The Gallant Captain was summoned to appear before the Council at Westminster, on a charge of interfering with justice. Cardinal Wolsey, however, was a friend of Vaughan.

Every time the case came up, he managed to quietly adjourn it till the next sitting. Incredibly, he kept this scam going for twelve years. Eventually, de Carteret, who had been stuck in London for all that time, exploded, shouting that he demanded justice. Wolsey tried to bluff it out, but he too had enemies. The Council, belatedly alert, ordered Wolsey's arrest. Young de Carteret received a lot of support. More petitions against Vaughan were sent from the Island listing his flagrant wickedness. These included murder and drawing wages for thirty-six soldiers that didn't exist. In 1529 came the sentence. He was removed from the Office of Governor. That was all!

The Council in Westminster planned to have two, carefully selected, eminent, local men to represent Jersey in Parliament. However, the day their letter was presented to the States was the same day that the eminent ones would have been taking their 'Seats in the House'. It was a non-starter, but the matter keeps coming up.

Repairs and improvements were still being carried out at Mont Orgueil, but this meant more taxes. Most people didn't like parting with their hard earned cash. The Jersey man was no exception. This led to the statement that local taxpayers were 'obstinate'. There were threats of imprisonment, so the money was shelled out eventually.

This was a time for culture and creativity to raise its head. The world was opening up, and Jersey was not far behind. First though came the Reformation. For years there had been calls for church reform. It was riddled with many abuses. Endowments were sold as investments. Positions of power were bought for sons or daughters. Court officials became Bishops and Canons. The Queen of Scotland's Chaplain who lived in Edinburgh was given the Priory of St Helier - and made sure his tenants paid the rent without delay.

In Europe the teachings of the church were also under fire. A new teaching of simple faith was superseding the theory that one must earn salvation by continuous church going, punishments and relentless God-bothering. Belief and trust in Christ. It was refreshing, simple, and it really caught on in Europe, and in Jersey - but then came the backlash!

The Sorbonne, founders of the Paris Theological Faculty, ordered the French translation of the Testament to be burned. Anyone caught reading it went to prison.

It did not take long before the believers, or non-believers, began to be executed. In 1523, victims of their new beliefs were burned to death in Paris and Meaux. Very soon more barbaric killings were introduced. Tongues were torn out with red-hot irons. Victims were lowered in and out of flames on pulleys to increase their agony.

There were no such atrocities in Jersey but word of the new thinking was causing ripples. In Europe, the movement for reform was driven underground as more priests and lay readers were thrown on the bonfire. It was only when a change of Government caused support to be withdrawn from the Secular Arm that the old Church system collapsed.

When Henry VIII died in 1547, his young son Edward came to the throne. King Edward VI was a serious, delicate lad just nine years of age. His uncle Hertford who was still Governor of Jersey now showed himself to be very anti-Catholic. He managed to get the old heresy laws thrown out. Next he tackled the practice of charging to say Mass for the dead. The new law forbidding this custom was passed in November 1547.

Because of this, many Priests were thrown out of work, but at least a pension was arranged for them. Several of the Chapels were turned into cottages.

A year later, a Royal command ordered the destruction of all objects of superstition. At this time Jersey was full of simple wood or granite wayside crosses. As soon as the command was received, the destruction of the crosses began. In no time these symbols, revered and bowed to by all who passed by, were rubble. Today only place names remind us of their location.

Most Rectors were in favour of the Reform movement. The few that were not, lost their jobs. Two French Protestant theologians were brought in to educate the locals into the new ways of God. They were remunerated by voluntary contributions of wheat from all Rectors and Jurats, paid at Michaelmas.

In 1549, it became legal for clergy to marry. The day after Henry II of France had been gushing to the English Ambassador about his love for all things English and the impossibility of war, he invaded and occupied Sark.

Eleven days later, thwarted in his attempt to take Guernsey, thanks to a stout defence by ships in the harbour, he sailed for Jersey. Their landing on July 31st at Jardin d'Olivet, may have seemed a good idea at the time, but the Jersey Militia had different ideas. The fighting was fierce and bloody. A Jurat and the Lieutenant Governor were killed but the French were beaten back, and retired hurt.

It was heard on the grapevine that one ship sailed into St Malo with more than sixty dead on board. Unfortunately they held on to Sark for the next nine years.

In March 1550, Sir Hugh Poulet was appointed Governor of Jersey for life. His finger was well and truly in the religious pie. A keen reformist, he continued the work of removing all signs and thoughts of Popery, 'so repugnant to the King.'

In France and England, this policy had caused rebellions and civil war but, strangely, in Jersey it was generally accepted. The very few protesters were fined and made to apologize. Rather unfair though, was the imprisoning of a man who 'allowed his wife to take a rosary with her to St Peter's Church'!

Sir Hugh continued the tradition of building and strengthening fortifications at Gorey, St Aubin and what became Elizabeth Castle. He sold the Church bells to pay for it all. This left just one bell in each Parish.

He had been instructed to move St Helier to the top of Mont De La Ville, where Fort Regent now stands, but this caused a problem. The town's people refused to leave their homes to live on that windy mound. The homes that folk were loath to abandon were usually built of granite, but with very little lime available, a substitute for mortar had been found. This was a mixture of clay, straw, bits of broken pots and animal hair. The 'mortar' worked very well except in heavy rain. If the mixture softened, the result would be a collapsing house!

These dwellings nearly always faced south. They comprised two up, two down and a box room over the front door. The staircase was stone, but most partitions were wood, unless you were very rich. Cooking and heating came from a massive granite fireplace. In 1552, Edward VII died. His elder sister Mary succeeded him, and brought about chaos.

The new Queen was a Catholic and she was determined to stamp out Protestantism.

In Jersey, the new Reformation was reversed. The services in Latin came back. Out went the Protestant Rectors and the sacked priests came back. Priests, who had married and now refused to leave their wives, were imprisoned on a bread and water diet. There were several floggings and threats of flogging.

Meanwhile, in England and even in Guernsey, people of all ranks were being burned at the stake.

Thankfully Jersey escaped this terrible penalty. This was due to the masterly way in which Poulet, walking a political tightrope, made it appear that all the Queen's commands were being carried out. He also made his brother Dean of Jersey. His brother was a Catholic, and between them, they were able to control the more bloodthirsty of the Church authorities.

In 1555 the Catholic cause took two heavy blows. The Dean's Proctor, Richard Averty, strangled and buried his maid's newborn baby. He was sentenced to be hanged. On the way to Gallows hill,

Westmount, the Dean tried to stop the execution by throwing a surplice over Averty's head and daring them to hang him, and claiming that he could only be tried by the Ecclesiastical Court. The Jurats were determined that the perpetrator of such a horrible crime should not escape the law. The surplice was torn away by the hangman and Averty swung from the scaffold.

The behaviour of the Dean raised more anti-Catholic feeling. When news arrived that Queen Mary was dead, the final blow had been struck. Elizabeth was Queen and Jersey reverted to the Protestant faith.

In 1561, there was yet another new Bailiff, Hostes Nicolle. His family came from Cornwall and owned Longueville Manor. His life was unremarkable, but the tale of his death is indeed strange.

Hostes Nicolle lived next door to a man who owned some land and property. Nicolle wanted it and, therefore took steps to obtain it. First he ordered some of his men to kill two of his best sheep and carry them to the neighbour's house. Next he called the Constable and the honorary police, reported a theft and pointed the finger next door. When the property was searched, there were the sheep hanging in the stable.

The poor man was arrested, taken to Court, found guilty and condemned to be hanged the same day. As the hangman placed the noose around his neck, the man turned to Bailiff Nicolle and said. 'I summon you to appear within forty days before the just Judge of all, to answer for this!' The wronged man died on the rope in the doorway of the Court. Thirty-nine days later, on his way back from town, Nicolle dropped dead at the roadside.

There was much to-ing and fro-ing at this time over which prayer book and order of service should be used, the commands and arguments went on and on. Someone then remembered the Bill of

1500 when the Pope had transferred the Island's religious scene to Winchester. Eventually the Council ordered the Channel Islands be separated forever from Coutances and permanently united with Winchester.

Of course the Bishop of Coutances got in a huff over this. He threatened to raise an army and take the Islands. But it all fell through.

Because of the frequent raids on Sark by pirates over the years, the Island had become de-populated. Rather than have an empty Island and an open invitation to foreign settlers, Helier De Carteret decided to rent it. He paid Queen Elizabeth 50 shillings (£2.50) a year and populated it with men from his own parish of St Ouen.

Meanwhile with the arrival of more Huguenots from France the Church became more powerful. Although the 'men in black' did distribute Alms to the poor, the regime became much stricter, at times even harsh. If you danced, played skittles or even gossiped on a Sunday, you ended up in the cells. Failing to say grace or to have household prayers each morning could get you reported to the Parish Elders. Rude jokes or saucy songs could cost you dear. It was very easy to get yourself excommunicated - and anyone who associated with you afterwards would suffer the same fate.

Naturally this was not acceptable to everyone. People rushed through the countryside at night wearing masks, carrying clubs, screaming obscenities and causing chaos. One of these, a girl wearing man's clothes, ended up in the stocks.

Devil worship and witches became fashionable. Many women and men were arrested. Several confessed, not under duress, but boastfully and full of defiance. Most were hanged. In Guernsey they were burned alive!

La Hougue Bie with Princes Tower.

St Brelade's Bay.

CHAPTER SIX
1600 - 1700

Around the 1600's, The Calvinist regime included a great care for education. Various schemes were set up to give financial help to lads that showed promise. This included sending them to Oxford.

At this time trade in the form of Newfoundland cod and a growing knitting industry was in full swing. Knitting was born of necessity but became big business and it caused a big problem.

Around 1600, fishermen and their families, to provide good snug-fitting jumpers for protection from the Atlantic gales, knitted Jerseys and Guernseys. They used locally gathered wool from locally gamboling, four horned, sheep. The Jersey had no gaps or pockets to catch in the fishing gear. The necks were said to be so tight so 'as to make the ears bleed'.

They were knitted 'on the round' using four needles. The jersey usually has a distinctive anchor design knitted into the pattern. They are still available, but no longer hand knitted by men of the sea. There was not much call to export these garments, as most fisher folk from Lands End to John O'Groats were knitting their own.

In Jersey, having got the hang of the needles, fishermen, farmers, their wives and their families, took up the latest European craze of knitting and exporting stockings. They took to it like ducks to water. Families Islandwide spent their days and evenings, singing and yarning to the busy click-click of the needles. Jersey is not really 'sheep country'. Very soon there was not an unshorn sheep to be seen. Wool was shipped in from Southampton, urgently, to keep the thousand knitters in business. As many as six thousand pairs were being exported each week, but here lay the problem!

Fish were not being netted, harvests lay unharvested and the Vraic (seaweed used for fertilizer) lay abandoned and rotting on the beach. When the authorities got wind of this, they got the needle!

Two new laws came into being: - (1) Thou shall not knit during harvest time; (2) The quality of the stockings must be maintained. No more two-ply yarn, three ply only.

With this quality control, Jersey Hose became famous throughout Europe. The Italians preferred them to their own which tended to rot! Even Mary Queen of Scots wore 'Jersey Hose white' on the day of her execution.

As the Island was still considered neutral, inhabited by weak labourers and poor fishermen, there were great opportunities for trade with both sides and good profits for Jersey.

Sir Amyas Poulet ruled Jersey but was often called away on the Queen's business, as a sort of travelling troubleshooter. During these absences his brother George stood in. When Sir Amyas died in 1588, his son Anthony got the job of Governor. The danger from Spain was still very real. The odd Spanish fleet tended to pop up occasionally.

Sir Anthony Poulett, The Governor Of Jersey from 1588 to 1600.

Anthony Poulet had decided to continue the work on Mont Orgueil castle that his father and grandfather had financed but then changed his mind. The Castle was overlooked 'by a mighty hill' and had little strategic value. It was not worth spending more cash on. A new castle was needed. Elizabeth Castle was conceived, built, armed and ready in just six years.

When in 1600, Anthony, or Sir Anthony as he became, died. Jersey received its most distinguished Governor - Sir Walter Raleigh. Here was a man who wore many hats, Soldier, Sailor, Poet, Chemist, Historian and Explorer, also Smoker and Potato importer!

These pastimes kept Sir Walter busy away from the Island. He tended his duties in Jersey for only five weeks over a period of two years. He was, however, in touch with events and, in the nick of time, slapped a preservation order on Mont Orgueil thus preventing it being torn down.

James I took the throne in 1603. This was the signal for the usual infighting and plotting. Somehow Sir Walter got stuck in the middle of it all. There were accusations of treachery. Jersey got a new Governor, John Peyton, whilst Sir Walter spent the next ten years in The Tower, sentenced to death.

As usual, Jersey was in a spate of ecclesiastical upheaval. Governor Peyton was in the middle trying to curb the Presbyterian jurisdiction over the Island. Royal commissions sat. In 1620, a Dean was appointed and the old 'Book of Discipline' was abandoned. It is interesting to note that in 1618, a comet was seen over the Island on twenty-two nights and a Sunday. Two church spires were struck by lightening and this was taken as a sign of displeasure from above.

The Dean, who was Italian, was never really accepted. In April 1620 he was sworn in. There was uproar in the States. For years Philippe de Carteret referred to him even in official documents, as 'One Bandinel, an Alien'!

Governor Sir John Peyton was a rather arrogant fellow and not the greatest believer in democracy. He complained that the Island's authorities failed to give support or to show obedience and respect.

In 1615 Jean Herault, a Jersey man who had 'served the King well', became Bailiff. His bank account was small but his ego was extremely large. He called himself 'High Bailiff' and gave himself the title of Monsieur de St Sauveur. He donned red robes and ordered the clergy, in prayers, to put his name before that of the Governor! That, and the fact that the Governor had been ordered to pay 100 marks per year to the man whom he considered to be an upstart, set the seal on their mutual hatred.

The next two years were a history of petty spites on both sides. The Bailiff would report the Governor to the Council for some imagined misdemeanor, and then the maligned Governor would retaliate in a similar vein.

In 1617, realizing that all was not well, the Council sent two Royal Commissioners over to get things sorted out. They found out that The Bailiff, Herault, though very vain and always irritable with an explosive temper, had two good points. His bark was worse than his bite and he was incorruptible, both unusual characteristics in those times.

They also found that his accusation that Peyton was depleting the Island's defenses to line his own pocket was true! One young fellow, Philippe Marette, Governor Peyton's right hand man, really showed himself up in front of the Commission. First he refused to deliver a necessary document to the Court, next he falsely accused them of trying to murder him. The Bailiff fined him 50 Crowns, which he refused to pay and he refused to apologize. He was suspended from his office and sent to appear before the Privy Council. They threw him into the gatehouse to cool off.

Later, he was sent back to Jersey to apologize and pay his fine. Amazingly he still refused to obey or behave, so Mont Orgueil got another tenant. Although he was treated very well in the Castle, he still whined to the Commission of his suffering, The Commission, in their wisdom, decided that he had brought everything on himself through his haughty and insolent behaviour. It would be nice to think that such an unpleasant individual languished there to this day, but somehow he managed to escape to England.

Meanwhile, our fiery Bailiff, Jean Herault, had fallen foul of the King. He refused to allow the Ecclesiastical court to elect Church Wardens. This was in defiance of the King's instructions. Herault was summoned to Westminster, lost his temper, and he was suspended. Later the King decided that having a fiery temper was not grounds for dismissal and the reinstated Bailiff returned to a hero's welcome from the whole States Assembly.

He died two years later, and it was said that his pig-headed attitude and obsession with both the dignity of his post and the status of Jersey, had secured us the right to self-government.

In 1626 eighteen-year-old Sir Philippe de Carteret filled the post of Bailiff. A year later, trouble was afoot, the French of course!

The young Bailiff had improved the fortifications at Elizabeth Castle and borrowed two hundred conscripts from England. Unfortunately most of them were rejects and ruffians. The locals were not impressed. When word came that the French had a fleet of one hundred and eighty vessels all set to attack the Island and just waiting for a favourable wind, panic ensued. An urgent cry for help was sent by letter to England, The envelope was marked HASTE! HASTE! HASTE! POST HASTE, HASTE FOR LIFE!

After all that the attack never came, and the French war ended in 1629. Despite that, all was not sweetness and light in the English

Channel. Spanish privateers based at Dunkirk posed a threat to shipping. On one occasion these pirates captured the Bailiff and the Dean of Jersey whilst they were returning to the Island. The ransom left young de Carteret almost broke.

Taking prisoners at sea and selling them as slaves was all the rage at this time. The Barbary pirates took twenty-seven vessels in under two weeks. In 1638, the States gave Nicolas Effart the almost impossible task of locating Jersey men who were held as slaves in Algeria. Amazingly, he returned with seventeen men, including his own brother!

In 1630 there was another Governor who, of course, left the job to his Lieutenant. This was an arrogant man who so misused his powers and continually got up people's noses that he was withdrawn. Philippe de Carteret became Lieutenant Governor as well as Bailiff.

The population of around twenty-five thousand, was divided roughly into four. The top two thousand or so Seigneurs with their huge families were very well off. The men swaggered around in suits trimmed with satin ribbons, gold buttons and pearl collars. There was a law passed forbidding the 'lower orders' to dress above their station.

Next were the farmers who had no money but had property, animals and land to supply their needs. This included home made clothing made from sheep's wool.

The amount that the few artisans, tailors, carpenters, etc. could charge was set. They were not allowed to raise their prices in case it caused inconvenience to their betters. In fact, even to ask for more was a punishable offence. A full day's work would buy a tailor a wild rabbit, whilst a stone mason's earnings would get him a pound of butter. The rest were casual labourers, paupers and beggars, and begging could land you in the stocks. There were no physicians, but the Rector would dose the sick with home made pills and potions.

When the plague of 1626 struck the Island, the death toll in St Brelade rose from nine a year to one hundred and thirty in just seven months. Because, understandably, no one wanted to carry the bodies to the cemetery, many of the victims were buried in their own gardens!

Philippe de Carteret was Bailiff, Lieutenant Governor, and Receiver General. Six close relatives held similar important positions and ten of the twelve Militia Captains were also part of the clan.

For twenty years, the King had granted The Dean, David Bandinel, certain monies and titles. Now suddenly Philippe, who hated the Dean, decided that the loot should be in his keeping and he demanded twenty years of back pay as well. As even his own Jurats wouldn't back him up on his claim, he kept dashing over to England and appealing to the Council. In the end his impudent demand was dismissed.

There was a move by some anti de Carteret Jurats, including Jurat Lempriere, to have some of his powers curtailed. After a great deal of underhanded dealing by his friends, plus a lot of luck, de Carteret triumphed and continued to rule over the Court. On one more occasion he attempted to prevent his enemy the Dean from taking his rightful seat, but his gambit failed.

In 1662,England plunged itself into civil war. Jersey would have preferred to remain neutral, but controversy is infectious and taking sides is a good way to repay old scores. Rumour ran rife, feeding fears and causing unease. Soon the Island became active against the Parliamentarians. Ships were captured en route for London. Parliament ordered the arrest of Philippe de Carteret, but as he commanded the local garrison, the five Jurats given the task of 'apprehending his person' were on a sticky wicket and, for the moment, left well alone!

There were dramatic scenes in the Court when a letter was read out demanding de Carteret's arrest. De Carteret, who read out a letter from the King, countered this. Arguments ensued, halberds were shaken and swords rattled but, when it was heard that the Militiamen from St Clement and St Aubin were marching to town and St Ouen was arming, Philippe de Carteret decamped rapidly to Elizabeth Castle with his guards.

There followed all sorts of shrewd schemes to have Philippe acquitted, like trying to make sure his friends were on the Royal Commission - but that one didn't work. He remained at the Castle. On one occasion he bombarded the town to intimidate what he called 'the rebels'. A bit of a commando raid was launched from the Castle. Creeping through the sand dunes, the men reached what is now called Charing Cross, they then heard that the tide had turned and they were about to be cut off. There was nothing for it, the commandos had to turn back.

Philippe and the Dean continued to trade insults and threats by letter! In the end, the Good Lord in his wisdom decided that enough was enough. Sickness broke out at Elizabeth Castle and Philippe de Carteret died in less than a month.

Both Mont Orgueil and Elizabeth Castle were still Royalist strongholds, so Parliament sent Leonard Lydcot, who held the rank equivalent to today's Lieutenant Colonel, to organize a siege or two.

Elizabeth Castle, now under the command of 'The Gentleman Porter' Hungerford, continued to bombard the town. One attack on market day caused extreme chaos and injury. Meanwhile night raids from Mont Orgueil gave the besiegers a difficult time.

Dean Bandinel offered to invite the committee of local Parliamentarians to dinner at St Mary's Rectory and have them taken prisoner! When Lydcot found out, the wily Dean had to go into hiding.

Everyone was getting tired of this pointless conflict. Many Militiamen decided to forget the siege and just went home. It was then that Sir George Carteret broke out from Mont Orgueil with a small army, many of whom had been shipped in from France. He marched across country and took the town. He didn't win the hearts of the people, as few would obey his order to swear allegiance to the King on the Bible. Despite becoming Bailiff and Lieutenant Governor, he still could not get Jersey men to fight for the King, nor would they agree to his scheme to attack and reclaim Guernsey for his Majesty.

Having grabbed any property vacated by his enemies and laid heavy taxes on everyone else, Sir George, still short of money, decided to do a bit of piracy. By capturing one ship, then using it to capture yet another and so on, he soon built up a small private fleet. Technically, as he and his men didn't have a 'Privateering license', they could all have swung at the yardarm as pirates, but in 1644 the King gave the go ahead by making him Vice Admiral of Jersey.

Apparently, most of the buccaneers who crewed his ships were non-Islanders and were disliked for their rowdy and unruly behaviour. 1645 saw the end of Dean Bandinel. He had been imprisoned in Mont Orgueil with his son for a year when rumour reached him that he was to be hanged by Sir George Carteret. They decided to escape. A great storm was raging as they squeezed through a narrow window and began to descend the wall on a rope made of knotted cords and towels. When the Dean was half way down the rope parted. Dean Bandinel died on the rocks below. His son who had gone first was captured next morning.

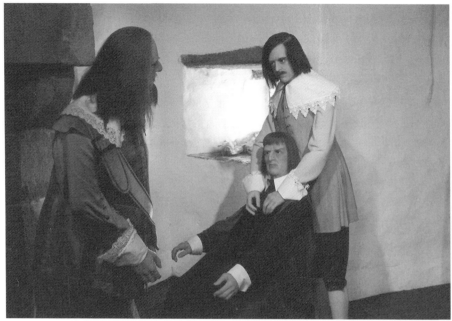

David Bandinel, the Dean of Jersey, imprisoned in Gorey Castle.

1645 was also revenge time and a Royal Commission arrived to try anyone who was accused of treason. They were an overbearing bunch, full of browbeating and threats. Their little gallop was curtailed when Parliament announced that for every so-called rebel they hanged, three Royalist prisoners would do likewise. They were still able to fine or imprison at will. Justice often had a low priority as Etienne La Cloch, Rector of St Ouen found out. Although he was a Royalist, Etienne had the temerity to criticize Carteret in public for his acts of piracy. As Carteret and the Royal Commission were in each other's pockets, his remarks earned the Rector eleven months in prison without heat or light. He could have earned his release by making a humble apology but, as a stubborn Jersey man, he flatly refused.

The expression 'Jobs for the Boys' was never truer than when, in 1646, King Charles I made his fifteen-year-old son, Prince Charles, 'Commander of our armies in the west'.Despite the importance of the title, his army was forced back and young Charlie along with a motley crowd of some three hundred Royalist hangers on and servants, was forced to flee to Jersey. Whilst finding accommodation for such a mob was difficult, the Prince set up in Elizabeth Castle where he dined off silver dishes surrounded by kneeling servants and canting clergy. Despite all this, Charles was always noted for his perfect courtesy, and his crooked smile.

Various plots were hatched to get hold of the Prince and thus enhance the cause of whoever had him in their clutches. An attempt to kidnap Charles and take him to Ireland was foiled. A message, supposedly from the King, urging him to go to his mother in France, was proved to be a forgery.

A plot to sell the Prince to Parliament helped him make up his mind. Prince Charles left for France accompanied by most of his Court.

In 1646 there was a complete change to the way of life in the Channel Islands. A devious fellow called Jermyn, thought he could help out his fellow ex-pat Royalists who were languishing in Paris. He would sell the Islands to France! There was uproar but luckily it all fell through. They couldn't agree upon a price!

A year later, the civil war in England had died down. The King was a prisoner and Parliament had their sights set on Jersey. The Island was sort of Royalist but not wholeheartedly. In fact if parliament had invaded, most ordinary Jersey folk would have welcomed them.

There was much wavering in Parliament about sending troops to 'reduce' Jersey, but there were all sorts of other problems to beset them on the home front. The King had been 'rescued' by the Army. The King had escaped from the army. The King was incarcerated on the Isle of Wight. Understandably, they forgot all about the Island.

Jersey of course had it's own problems too, mainly paupers and beggars. Compassion ruled and strenuous efforts were made to solve the problems of these unfortunates. The lower orders were not allowed to marry unless they were able to prove their ability to support a family, and Carteret provided a town house as a 'House of Correction'. This was to provide bread and water lock-up for unlicensed beggars, drunkards and able-bodied men caught knitting. As it was, the idea came to nothing. The States accepted the building but had no wish to pay for its maintenance. Instead they built an impressive new granite Court House emblazoned with the coats of arms of The King, the Governors, Carteret and the Bailiff. Masons were brought in from France for this important work.

Witch trials were still all the go, and in 1648, seven unfortunate ladies were prosecuted. Amazingly the trials were extremely fair for those times. There were twenty-four Jurors and, of them, nineteen would have to find the accused guilty in order to secure a conviction. Of the seven 'witches' one was flogged, and after evidence was heard from over seventy witnesses, two were executed in the Market place.

Meanwhile, Sir George Carteret tried to arrange the rescue of King Charles from the Isle of Wight, but the King decided to stay put. Undeterred, George decided it would be fun to invade Guernsey on behalf of the Royalists. Guernsey's Castle Cornet was still held by the Royalists and George Carteret planned to sort out the rest of the pro-Parliament island. However, the Governor of Castle Cornet did not trust George and, in effect, told him to push off.

Next came a plan to use force to recapture Sark, but a great storm blew up and put paid to his Sark lark!

Yet another cunning plan by Sir George to release the King from his new prison, Hurst Castle, was thwarted when Charles I was hastily removed to Windsor, and then to Westminster where he was beheaded.

Totally ignoring the fact that Parliament had abolished the office of 'King', and threatened death to all who disagreed, Sir George ordered Prince Charles to be proclaimed King Charles II .This act, in 1649, began his reign eleven years early, in Jersey anyway.

With few places to run to, Charles arrived in Jersey. Time hung heavy on the King's hands. He spent his time shooting rabbits and attending functions and though he was not noted for great abilities, he did possess the gift of healing. He cured twenty-four people of scrofulous, a nasty glands' problem.

In 1650, Charles II left the Island for Breda with a few of his entourage. Before he went, he presented Sir George with a group of islands called Smith Islands. These were a barren cluster of rocks off the Virginian coast. Carteret promptly renamed them New Jersey.

Afraid that Cromwell would attack Jersey, Carteret had hired mercenaries and privateers from several countries. They were the dregs and the cause of problems, not only to locals, but also to passing ships. Dozens were attacked and captured by what were, unfairly, known as the Jersey Pirates. Cromwell of course attacked.

For two days the fleet of some eighty ships sailed back and forth from St Ouen, round the point to St Brelade and then back again. For two days and nights Carteret's Militia, many of whom had no argument with Parliament anyway, marched and counter marched across country trying to anticipate the landing. The lads were fed up and even considered shooting Carteret.

When the landing came at 11pm it was still fiercely contended, but the outcome was a foregone conclusion. After all that tramping around the countryside, soaking wet and with little food, the exhausted men were forced back, finally retreating to St Aubin's Fort. Later when approached, the Jersey men in the garrison refused to bear arms against Parliament and opened the doors. By the following evening Cromwell's forces had taken the Island except for Mont Orgueil and Elizabeth Castle.

Mont Orgueil was well stocked with food, ammunition and troops, but the defenders had lost heart in the lost cause of the King. They were offered good terms if they surrendered the castle. The keys were handed over and they marched out with the full honours of war.

Now Elizabeth Castle stood alone as a Royalist stronghold.

The Commander of the Parliamentary forces, Colonel James Heane, had no intention of messing about. Three huge mortars were brought over from Portsmouth and set up at the foot of Town Hill.

They were capable of firing, or lobbing, a bomb containing forty pounds of gunpowder. The third shot went through the roof of the old church, blew up the castle's supply of gunpowder, destroyed most of the provisions and killed forty soldiers.

Young King Charles, who was sheltering in France was unable to raise money for fresh supplies and advised that Carteret negotiate a surrender. It took just eight days. He got excellent terms for himself and his family. They had total freedom and were allowed to retain all their property. His supporters did not fare so well. They had to hand over two years' income or have their property confiscated.

Elizabeth Castle was handed over and Sir George Carteret cleared off to join the French navy! The occupying forces were not all angels. The Red Coats were well disciplined and not too prone to liberating people's possessions, but they did not believe in the sanctity of the church. They burnt pews on their cooking fires and used the churches as guardrooms and toilets.

The five hundred men brought in from Guernsey to help in the invasion stole everything they could lay hands on. Their Commander, Major Harrison, was furious but he was unable to control them.

At the same time, people exiled by the Royalists came rushing back seeking revenge and property. This led to wrangles, petitions and threats.

Gradually things began to settle. The Bailiff was reappointed, trade recommenced and, despite the occupation, life went on. In 1652 and again in 1653, Westminster decided that Jersey would become just another English county or constituency with a local representative being sent to sit in Parliament. On both occasions the order was completely ignored by the Island.

Both Jersey and Guernsey shared the privilege of being exempt from the press gang, but despite it being illegal, they still tried it on. On one occasion, the press gang was set upon by the crowd whilst trying to 'press' men.

In St John, a man was shot dead by a soldier and his companions attacked with swords because they queried the Red Coats' right to press men into the forces.

The new Commander of the occupying force, Colonel Robert Gibbon, held all civilian officials in utter contempt. He thought nothing of throwing them into prison for any opposition to his orders.

In 1659, after the death of Cromwell, twenty-four articles of impeachment against the Colonel were sent to the New Reformed Long Parliament.

In January 1660, Old George Monk, Commander of the army in Scotland, marched south; opposition was swept aside. A month later, he entered London and sat Charles II on the throne.

The rule of the Red Coats in Jersey was at an end. It was May 8th, a date which is familiar to Channel Islanders!

The usual in fighting between the religious factions continued unabated. Men were punished for not removing their hats in church, or for calling the Anglican service a 'Mass'. A girl was punished for wearing male clothes at a masquerade.

In 1666, Louis XIV of France decided to declare war on England. As Jersey was in the firing line, we got a new Governor. Sir Thomas Morgan was a first class soldier. He re modelled the Jersey Militia, training them hard, never sparing them or him. He got Elizabeth Castle's fortifications rebuilt and strengthened, but to no avail, peace broke out within the year!

Sir Thomas also enjoyed being a thorn in the flesh of all local officials. When the Court forbade the importing of cider, just to be difficult, he had sixty hogsheads of cider shipped in and sold it to the Islanders.

Proper harbours were nonexistent. A pier was urgently required at St Aubin but, as usual, there were delays and petty squabbles. Sir Thomas offered to organize the job himself. With him in charge, the work went apace. In 1675, it was described as 'A piece for eternity'.

Through lack of commerce and various wars, paupers and begging became an epidemic. Various ideas were put forward to solve the problem, but Sir Thomas Morgan's was typical. Export them all to Ireland or New Jersey! In a spirit of Christian charity and compassion, the States agreed but the Council, however, did not. Many Jersey men and women did in fact make new lives in America.

The direct trade with America in cod, rum, molasses, wines, shoes and Jersey stockings, took a bad knock in 1651 with the new 'Navigation Act'. This act prevented the importation of merchandise except in English ships. Jersey merchants who flouted this penny-pinching law lost both ship and cargo.

Sir George Carteret was now back on the scene. A great believer in education, he decided to found some scholarships. This was achieved, but not before Dean Prideaux of Oxford, suggested in a letter that, 'It will be hard to find a college for brutes'.

When Sir Thomas Morgan died in 1679, Sir John Lanier, another man who enjoyed quarrelling with the States, succeeded him. He vetoed the out-of-pocket expenses of The Vicomte, who retaliated by having Lanier's garden wall pulled down, stating that it might make a gun site if anyone decided to bombard Elizabeth Castle!

In those days, there would have been no 'having a lie in' and a leisurely brunch on a Sunday. The Laws on Sabbath breaking were fierce. The head of the household was fined if he or any of his family, or his servants, failed to attend the church service. Surprise visits were paid on homes during church time in the hopes of catching the un-Godly. The result was large congregations and excellent opportunities for burglars!

In 1685 Charles II was dead. The States sent the new King, James II, an effusive and fawning letter. Meanwhile Louis IV got married. His wife was a 'big Catholic' with a resulting dislike of Protestants. She suggested that it was time, and his duty, to persecute them. Louis began this assignment by billeting his dragoons in Protestant houses - with permission to behave as badly as they liked! He banned all Protestant worship and pulled down Huguenot temples. This led to the exodus from France of around half a million people, several thousand arrived in Jersey, bringing the skills of many craftsmen and playing leading roles in Island life.

Smuggling to France and England from Jersey had become a growth industry. One Customs officer, who was sent to put a stop to it, complained that the whole Island was against him, including the authorities! When he tried to do his job he was often clobbered and insulted. In the end the poor fellow did the only sensible thing, he joined them.

James II, began to introduce Popery into England and, unwisely, Jersey. An Irish Catholic Lieutenant Governor, a Deputy, several Chaplains and extra troops, all from the Emerald Isle, arrived on our sandy shores. In November 1688, James of Holland landed in England. James II pushed off hurriedly. Mary Stuart and husband William of Holland were proclaimed King and Queen. The Catholic influence was still strong in the Island, and there was fear that they might allow the predominantly Catholic French to invade. There were many rumours and accusations of plots and Popery. In the end, a regiment of English troops, under the Earl of Bath, arrived. The Catholic element was disarmed and the Island was back to the normal Protestant squabbling.

In 1689, England was at war with France. The Channel Islands were still considered neutral, but they rather blew it by trading with France, using the Ecréhous as a meeting point cum trading post. This was frowned upon by the King. However, as the trade was very profitable and as the Lieutenant Governor was heavily involved, the King's frowns were ignored.

The late 1600's seemed to be a time for the people to start questioning their so called betters, especially when it came to the shooting of rabbits. Did the Seigneurs have exclusive rights over land occupied by tenants? The dispute went to the Court and the tenants won the day. They had the right to bag a few rabbits for the pot. In St Ouen, the tenants revolted against the annual dues and duties levied by their Seigneur. Supplying cartloads of vraic (seaweed for fertilizer), the collecting of wood and stone for building plus supplying manual labour, all free of charge, seemed a bit much to the Jersey man. A twelve-man commission was set up, but they found against the tenants. This was not the end of the matter in St Ouen. There were accusations, arrests and dismissals from office, followed by reinstatements.

Seigneur de Carteret then claimed that as his tenants had refused to pay their dues, their land was forfeited. The Dean and several Jurats laid complaints against the Seigneur. One being that he lived mainly in England and didn't understand Jersey law. Seigneur de Carteret played every trick in the book to confuse the issue but, in the end, the Council decided he was in the wrong. This was a great blow to his pride. He died in 1715.

CHAPTER SEVEN
1700 - 1800

When Sir Charles de Carteret died, John Carteret automatically filled the office of Bailiff. There was no election; it was just kept in the family.

Needless to say the bickering between the clergy and the laity continued unabated.

The Dean, Clement Le Couteur, excommunicated the Constable of St Peter and the Churchwardens for refusing to provide wine for Christmas Communion. Rather unfairly, as they had already laid it on for four other celebrations in the year. However the Dean overdid it a bit when he laid the charges against the Constable and the Wardens. His violent rhetoric landed him in prison for 'issuing scandalous statements'.

In 1704, the Bishop of Winchester complained about the behaviour of the laity toward the clergy in Jersey. The men in black were often insulted in public and sometimes even assaulted. He alleged that 'inferior sort of people' threw stones at them and at the Dean! In his complaint he laid blame for this behaviour firmly at the door of the Bailiff and Jurats who 'daily showed contempt for the clergy'. The Rector of St Helier apparently 'uttered many calumnious words against the honour of the Lieutenant Governor'. His sharp tongue led him straight to prison. Two years later, the Rector of St Ouen landed in jail for speaking out of turn. He maligned the Queen's officers. Seemingly freedom of speech was not a top priority!

Next, what might be referred to as the squabble over the pew with a view broke out at St John's church. Briefly, Mr Le Couteur enlarged his pew. Mr Ahier, whose view had been obstructed, complained to the Ecclesiastical Court. They ordered that the offending pew be removed. Mr Le Couteur appealed to the Royal

Court. They told Mr Ahier the pew should remain. Mr Ahier complained to the Dean, so the Court sent him to prison for two years. The Dean excommunicated Mr Le Couteur and ordered that notice of his decision should be read from every pulpit. The Royal Court forbade this. The Rectors read it out anyway and were all fined. Probably much of this is accounted for by pews being much sought after as status symbols.'

1709 was a time of general discord. Everyone from the Bailiff and clergy down to tenants, landlords and neighbours were in contention over something. It was also a time for questioning the powers of the States.

The restrictions they imposed certainly seem to swing between petty and draconian. The import of corn, wine and tobacco was restricted. The building of houses and the planting of orchards were subject to regulations. Knitted stockings could only be sold for money, it was a crime to barter them for goods.

Complaints about Court fees and the method of assessing fines were also to the fore. Farmers complained that Seigneurs kept so many rabbits and pigeons, just for the pleasure of shooting them, that crops were being ruined.

Another grouse was that many Jurats were very elderly, sick with the gout or just past it. The result being they could never get enough of them together at one time to try court cases. It was not until the early twentieth Century that an age limit of seventy-five was set.

Despite these storms in a bean-crock, overseas trade was expanding. This was mainly due to the expertise of Philippe Pipon and a few other merchant adventurers. Exotic imports from Spain and Lisbon were arriving in the Island. (Oranges, figs, lemons and raisins could now be enjoyed)

Trade with Newfoundland was tricky and dangerous. French and Spanish privateers roamed the waters in search of prey. Nevertheless, many young Jersey men travelled to the land of opportunity to become apprentices for several years. They received no wages, just bed, wholesome food and clothes. They received a modest education and, of course, learned a trade. Some of the earlier settlers had become merchants and planters. Others were well involved in shipping dried cod in all directions.

Meanwhile local merchants and entrepreneurs traded worldwide dealing in many currencies. They built themselves impressive homes, played the stock market and 'lived the life of Riley' in London and the fashionable resorts. This new elite made 'good marriages'. The offspring were sent off to mainland schools to be 'Englished'.

Of course ships were lost or severely damaged at sea and naturally pirates continued to earn their keep. After several local ships had lost their cargoes to privateers, Jersey sailors began to arm their ships and fight back.

Communication was a slow business in those days. In May 1734, Charles Pinel, captain of the hundred ton brigantine Seaflower, died of the plague whilst docked in Cyprus. It was eight years before the owners, a consortium of Jersey businessmen were traced and the ship released to them.

Another to be 'taken' by the plague a few years earlier, was Captain Philippe Janvrin. He died within sight of his home on board the Esther whilst the ship was quarantined off Noirmont point. The poor Captain was buried on the little isle in Portelet bay, now Janvrin's tomb.

In the early 1700s, the monetary system was a nightmare. Livres, tournois, liards, sous, sols, and deniers all rattled round in the Jersey man's pocket. This was a mixture of local and French currencies in copper, silver or gold. The values fluctuated and, whilst the wily Jersey merchants usually made a modest profit on an exchange, the wily French were getting more of our gold and silver.

When the States realised that the Island's gold was gradually draining away, they sprang into action. Several decrees forbidding the exporting or importation of various coinage were ignored.

The States sat on the situation for three years then, with permission from the Council, passed an order which became known as the six-au-sou. This law devalued the liard, the most used coin in the Island. No one had realized what was about to happen but, when the cat was let out of the purse, the Island went wild. Suddenly, hard earned savings were worth one third less. The people felt that the States had picked their pockets.

Reaction was so fierce that the States took fright. In November 1729 they sent the Constable of St Lawrence to the Privy Council, asking permission to revoke the law. The Bailiff, the Dean, the Attorney General and Jurat Dumaresq were all in favour of the six-au-sou so they too headed for Westminster. They opposed the U-turn and won the day. The order would be enforced, but delayed for six months.

A group of merchants petitioned the States saying that the Island would be totally ruined. They offered to find an alternative solution to the problem. Their suggestions fell on deaf ears.

It was on Saturday, August 29th that the Deninciateur began to publish the order in the Market Square. That Sunday saw the start of the biggest riot in the Island's history.

Tempers flared and stones flew. The Bailiff's house, where De Gruchy & Co now stands, was attacked and the windows shattered. A mob of three hundred angry Jersey men and women threatened to kill him and Jurat Dumaresq. A young Advocate, also named Dumaresq, calmed them down, saying wait till the States sitting on Monday.

The Lieutenant Bailiff, Le Geyt, appealed for help from the Lieutenant Governor. The tough old Colonel told Le Geyt he had brought it all on himself, but he did provide soldiers to guard his now windowless home.

Worship that Sunday was followed by heated debates and angry gatherings in the Island's churchyards. A mass demonstration was organized for the next day.

As the church bells began to ring on the Monday morning, the militia drummers marched through the parishes. Every man aged between eighteen and seventy was called upon to march on the town. They came from the North, the East and the West. St Ouen alone provided five hundred.

As the mass of angry men approached St Helier armed with cudgels, pitchforks and corn flails, the States called an emergency meeting. In what must be a record for the quickest decision ever made in the States, the law devaluing the liard was revoked, but the crowd neither believed nor trusted the authorities. The mob burst into the Court House yelling death to the six-au-sou. One old woman shrieked 'we'll have their guts, and I've brought a bag to put them in'.

The members who had pushed the law through originally, beat a hasty retreat. Several of them crawled under the benches to reach the back door. The Dean ran to a tavern, disguised himself in the taverner's greatcoat and cap, jumped out of a rear window and escaped to Elizabeth Castle.

The crowd was particularly angry with the Constable of St Lawrence because he was the one sent to Westminster to get the six-au-sou law set aside, but in the end he had agreed to it. He escaped by the skin of his teeth, stole a horse and also made a wild dash for the Castle!

Advocate d'Auvergne, the Bailiff's son-in-law, alone defied the wrathful horde. He stood his ground shaking a horsewhip at them and growling his support for the six-au-sou.When someone hit him across the legs and another knocked his wig off, his resolve faded. He ran for it; leaving the jeering, stick throwing crowd behind.

When the Lieutenant-Bailiff and the Lieutenant Governor, Colonel Howard, left the Court House, Le Geyt was sworn at and punched. Colonel Howard was also struck when he attempted to protect him. The decision to run for their lives was unanimous and prudent. Glancing back they saw a man with a raised grappling iron in hot pursuit. They just made it to the Colonel's house in one piece!

After a few days, Le Geyt slipped over to Guernsey. He knew he'd had a lucky escape. No way could he risk living in Jersey ever again. He wrote a letter resigning his post as Bailiff, but that was not the end of the sad six-au-sou saga!

King George II and his Privy Council were not pleased. The Jersey States should not have caved in to the mob. The ex Bailiff and some associates went to London to explain their dilemma. However, his Majesty felt that in cancelling the law, the States had 'insulted his Royal Authority'. He ordered that the six-au-sou law be reinstated immediately. To back his decision, George II sent Colonel Hargrave with four hundred men to the Island. Of course they were billeted on the long suffering inhabitants.

Predictably, the Lieutenant Governor, Col Howard, who had protected the Bailiff from the mob, was found guilty of not maintaining his Majesty's Royal Authority. He lost his job.

Although his Majesty had rebuked Jersey, several Jurats still had the audacity to vote against his command.

In June 1731, the Court decided the order should be translated into French and proclaimed in every parish. In St Martin, when the Provost attempted to proclaim it at the church door, he was knocked down and his proclamation destroyed.

A St Helier man was arrested for saying that if they were unwise enough to publish the order, 'the town shall be destroyed'! At long last, an opposition party of five Jurats 'came out of the closet'. Two pro six-au-sou Jurats died. There was an election and two new Jurats opposed to the law were voted in to take their place. One could have some sympathy with the complaints that the election was neither secret nor democratic. It seems that anyone voting for a pro six-au-sou candidate had a large cross chalked on his back to expose him to the fury of the crowd.

There was uproar in the Court as more 'points of law' were raised in an attempt to prevent the swearing in of the elected candidates. They were sworn in just the same and their party had, at last, the majority they needed. Their first act was to get all 'rioters' released from jail.

They still needed to get the majority of states members on their side. This was accomplished by a masterly stroke. They resurrected a long forgotten law, which stated that the parish Constables, twelve in all, could not serve for more than three years without re-election. Most of the Constables, who had been 'sitting' for around twenty years, had to retire.

The newly elected States decided once and for all to squash the six-au-sou order. The value of the liard went back to normal. This remained till 1834 when the new English monetary system was brought in. Now all was sweetness and light, but in Jersey nothing stays that way for long.

Tithes, a tenth of what you grew, belonged to the King and were paid over in goods, but his Receiver had unwisely decided to rent out the parishes to speculators. These entrepreneurs paid a lump sum down, which no doubt pleased his Majesty, then took the farmers for everything they could get their hands on.

There were always disputes as to the value of goods and a law had been passed ordering the payments to be in cash only. Unfortunately, this law had been accidentally axed in the confusion of revoking the six-au-sou. The Farmers were not happy. They demonstrated their unhappiness to the collectors of the tithes in subtle ways.

In St Ouen, the collector had his wall broken down, his oxen let loose in his cornfield and his front gate smashed. Death threats were nailed to his front door and his horse and an ox were shot! A mob of two hundred attacked the St Brelade farmers who were tithe collectors. They forced them out of their houses, beat them up and tore up their tithe contracts. In different parts of the Island, boats were untied and allowed to run onto the rocks. Corn ricks and fruit trees were damaged and there were more death threats.

Again the King was displeased. Some Jurats were dismissed for not punishing the rioters. The Court sittings were by now in such a disorganized mess, that two people, at least, reaped the benefit.

In 1736, Mary Le Maistre and John Bishop, who had awaited trial in prison for the last three years for the alleged murder of their child, were now released. There was no chance of getting a Court together to try their case. Understandably the Council got fed up with the Island's internal squabbles.

Gradually order was restored. The Courts were sorted out and the excitement died down, but in Jersey, memories are long. Even ten years later, the devaluing of the liard was not forgotten. A choice and provoking insult was to call someone a six-au-sou voter - or cochon!

In 1737, the foundation stone of the first public library was laid in Library Place. This was thanks to an aging Philippe Falle who donated two thousand books plus some money to the project. They moved it to the States buildings in 1866 and around a hundred years later it arrived at new premises in Halkett Place.

Halkett Place.

In 1741, Marie Bartlett of St Aubin left money to the poor. More importantly, she left money for the building of a poor house, mainly for the benefit of widows and orphans. This was eventually to become the General Hospital.

Located on the sand hills to the west of St Helier, it began to take shape, after objections from her relatives, in 1765. As soon as the building was finished, it was requisitioned as an Army barracks. It was not long before some 'horrible little man did something unwise in the gunpowder store'. Half the building blew up! Eventually it was rebuilt, but before the patient queue of widows could take possession, six thousand Russian troops arrived and were moved in. Apparently they were cut off from home by ice in the Baltic and although they were allies, for political reasons, they were not allowed on English soil. It is said that 'the officers charmed the local ladies with their balls and dinner parties, but the shaggy privates were not so popular'!

These privates apparently ate the Island's supply of tallow candles and drank all the lamp oil.

In 1854 the place was gutted by fire. Again it was rebuilt and became the General Hospital. Even in 2006 it is, like the Forth Bridge, still being refurbished.

Ever fearful of invasion from France, a sort of 'quallies' law was introduced in 1763. An order forbidding any foreigner of the Roman church from living in Jersey or marrying a local girl was passed. 'Having Quallies' is a 90s slang expression for our immigration controls.

They also decided to build fortifications around the Island. The work was still going on three years later but it was proving expensive and very difficult. More regiments were drafted in and the drain on local resources became impossible. At this point the King agreed to foot the bill for the lot.

In 1669, Suzanne Dumaresq got permission to build a corn market exchange in the Market square with dwelling above for herself. The United Club now owns this and part is the Registrar's office. The Chamber of Commerce building, on the opposite side of the square, was the site of a cage used for containing prisoners awaiting transfer to the dungeons of Mont Orgueil after being sentenced in the Court. In 1751 a statue of George II of gilded lead was erected in the Market Square, it was protected by railings. The Market Square became the Royal Square.

The Market Square became the Royal Square.

Pioneering Jersey men were trading far and wide. Buying, selling, and privateering. One rich and influential merchant, Joshua Mauger, left a small fortune to his nephew, whose own son Philippe Nicolle, built an impressive town house behind the family shipbuilding yards - here stands the Jersey Museum.

Philippe Nicolle's was not the only boat-building yard. The first Jersey-built ship of note was the 280 ton 'Tupper'. It was constructed near the south end of St Peter's Valley, using good Jersey oak. It was launched in June 1789.

It was suggested in La Gazette that there was enough woodland in the Island to provide timber for the building of all the ships that were needed. The Jersey man is ever ready to earn a bob or two and be self-sufficient. In no time, boat yards were being set up in all directions. This also gave work to sail makers, Carpenters, Coopers, and Blacksmiths. Occasionally you may come across a 'rope walk' in the Island - there is one behind Fort Regent. These were long straight areas where ropes for the ship's riggings were laid out and stretched.

The importance of protecting our ever-growing trade was, in 1768, reflected by the setting up of a Chamber of Commerce, the first in the English-speaking world!

The post of Bailiff had become hereditary in the de Carteret family, but it was sixty years since they had bothered even to visit the Island. In 1750, Charles Lempriere became Lieutenant Bailiff. The Governor also left everything to his ever-changing Lieutenants. One such, a Colonel Ball, was described as having no more intelligence than an oyster, and, similar to that shellfish, only opened his mouth to take in fluids! This meant that Lt. Bailiff Lempriere had a complete free hand in running Jersey's affairs, which was a dangerous situation!

At this time, the Royal Court ruled the roost. The twelve Jurats were autocratic and totally unsympathetic to the lot of the man in the street. Of these, five were related to the very autocratic Lt. Bailiff. In 1758, his brother became Attorney General. The way was open for Charles Lempriere to become a dictator. Totalitarian laws were introduced through the Court. The same Court punished protesters. Resentment grew.

The Lemprieres cheated farmers out of their land, even sold a ship they didn't own, but still continued to prosper. There was resentment too at the appalling way Lempriere had treated French prisoners during the seven-year war. They slept on filthy straw and were only fed twice a week.

Nicholas Fiott, a sea Captain, was loud in his complaints against the Lt. Bailiff and his blunt remarks led to his arrest. In Court he objected to four of the Jurats trying him. When he put his feelings rather strongly in writing, he was ordered to ask pardon of God, the King and the Bench on his knees! His refusal landed him in a cell. Such a huge petition was mounted for his release that the Privy Council ordered him to be bailed. Meanwhile there were still murmurings of discontent within the Island, particularly as food was now in short supply. In 1767 ship owners were threatened with violence if they dared to load food for export. Although the States forbade the export of corn, a year later they rescinded the order. It was to the benefit of investors that the price of corn stayed high to increase their profits, but this put up the price of bread. The people were not happy. A mob of women raided a ship and sold the cargo of corn on the docks. Amazingly they did reimburse the owners!

Once again, armed with stout sticks, stones and quite a few demands, Jersey was on the march! Once more an angry crowd invaded the Courthouse. They assaulted the usher and made blood-curdling offers to the Magistrates. The protesters occupied the building for five hours during which several new acts were compiled and hurriedly voted in!

For the next few days, things went quiet, but deviousness was afoot! Two of the Lemprieres went to Westminster. They appeared before the Council all bedraggled and scruffy, claiming to have just escaped the mob in the clothes they stood up in! In fact they had been resting happily in Elizabeth Castle for three days. They painted a harrowing picture of bloodthirsty rioters, demanding that the King's laws be erased from the statute book. As expected His Majesty threw a wobbly and sent five Companies of the Royal Scots to sort out the revolting Islanders.

Their Commander, Colonel Bentinck, a shrewd man, soon realised that injustice was the cause of the trouble. Eventually the

Colonel was made Governor, with orders to pacify the Islanders. Although Lempriere's power had waned, amazingly he still had his supporters. The Island was now split into two political parties. The 'Charlots' who supported Charles Lempriere, and the 'Jeannots' - also nicknamed the maggots by the opposition, who followed Jean Dumaresq. He was a brilliant speaker and sworn enemy of Charles Lempriere. Every election became a no holds barred battle. No stunt was considered too illegal, no trick too low, in order to win the day. Bribery was rife. Voters were made too drunk to reach the polls. There were cases of voters being kidnapped and dumped out on the Ecréhous for the day. Eventually, Jean Dumaresq and his maggots gained the upper hand and Lempriere resigned.

In 1778 England and France were at loggerheads again. Martello towers begin to appear along the Island's coast and, naturally, Jersey's privateers were ready to take full advantage. With mounted swivel guns at the ready, these licensed Jersey pirates preyed on the French shipping in the Channel and Biscay. There were rich pickings. On one occasion these bold rascals even landed near Caen, and 'liberated' several cows, sheep and oxen. They also pinched the Cure's washing and abducted his housekeepers. The French planned retribution. An attempted landing at St Ouen was a fiasco. None of the French Captains would sail close enough to the shore because of an ebbing tide. There was much Gallic chatter whilst the Jersey Militia waited patiently to receive their 'Guests'. The tide got lower, the invasion was aborted and the French sailed majestically for home. On the way, the English navy, who added to their discomfort, met them!

No one took notice of the nondescript sailor from the grain boat as he wandered around on the beaches. Had they known that he was Baron de Rullecourt spying out the land, they might have been concerned. The Battle of Jersey was imminent, but only he knew that.

On January 5th, 1781 at midnight, the Baron led his flotilla of boats through the two-mile stretch of jagged rocks at La Rocque. It would have been a hazardous and almost impossible journey to undertake but de Rullecourt had help. A Jersey man named Journeaux who had escaped from the Island to avoid the hangman's rope, had returned to guide the Islands enemies. Carefully he took them through the narrow channel known only to local fishermen. The Baron had worked on the assumption that the militia would be less than alert over the festive season, and he was right. The French crept ashore unseen. Leaving behind a hundred men to guard their landing place, the Baron and his small army marched on the town.

The sun wasn't even up when Jersey's Lieutenant Governor, Major Corbet was awakened with news of the invasion. Before he could decide if it was just an awful nightmare, the French were on his doorstep and he was a prisoner. It was at this point that Baron de Rullecourt very nearly won the day with guile and bluff!

Actually the Baron only had six hundred men, and they were in the Royal Square. He persuaded a confused Major Corbet that another four thousand surrounded the town and ten thousand would be arriving that evening. He explained to the poor Lieutenant Governor that half the troops in the Island had already surrendered. He threatened that if he, Corbet, did not sign an order for the complete surrender of the local garrison, he would burn down St Helier. Caught between a rock and a hard place and, unwisely believing a Frenchman, he signed the order.

Baron de Rullecourt began issuing dinner invitations to local dignitaries, but Captain Aylward in Elizabeth Castle ignored the order and his men fired on any French soldiers that approached. Captain Mulcaster, typically English, returned the order saying he didn't understand French.

The Highlanders and several Militia units rallied on Gallows Hill, (Westmount) whilst Major Francis Peirson marched the 95th foot to join them. Major Peirson was given command of the force, some 1,600 men but there was a problem. Could the young Major disobey the written orders of Corbet, his Commander in Chief? Corbet was taken out under the white flag to parley. He ordered Major Peirson to surrender his troops. The Major told his Commander that he would rather die than surrender and gave him just ten minutes to clear off!

The French were massed in the Royal Square. Major Peirson sent troops up to Town Hill (now Fort Regent site). From there they were able to pour a withering fire down on the packed Square over the roof of the old Court building. Meanwhile, as his main force advanced up Broad Street and Library Place, the Major took another party up Rue de Derriere (King Street) and burst into the Square through what is now Peirson Place.

The Battle of Jersey was over. The French were defeated but, as the smoke cleared, Major Peirson and Baron Rullecourt, both brave and gallant men, lay dead.

At La Rocque, the Rector of St Martin and Captain Campbell of 'The Glasgows' attacked and overpowered the remaining French troops. A stone in Grouville churchyard commemorates this action.

The Battle of Jersey in the Royal Square.

The scene at La Rocque.

Overlooking St Helier and Gallows Hill, (Westmount).

The two political parties were still at it hammer and tongs, each trying to out do the other in childish behaviour and low tricks. The first local paper, Le Magasine de Ille de Jersey hit the streets in 1784. It was a monthly publication costing 6d (2p). Dumaresq's brother financed it. It was very pro Maggot! The proprietor, Mathieu Alexandre, was very outspoken and tended to criticize loudly. He was taken to Court and released on bail so many times, that 'Le Magasine' folded in just over a year.

However, in 1786, it rose from the ashes as The Gazette, a weekly newspaper under the same management. This gained much support and could not be gagged. It was to thrive for fifty years.

Politics was still a ding-dong battle. The Gazette printed one-sided versions of States sittings and generally stirred things up. By 1790, Dumaresq's party had gained a majority in the Court and in the States. That year Lempriere died.

With the French revolution raging a few miles away, danger from that quarter was considered to be very real. More fortifications were needed urgently, but how were they to be paid for? A lottery was held on January 24th, 1789. Amid great excitement the first ticket was drawn 'out of the wheel' by two lads dressed in blue with red sashes. They were accompanied by two Jurats in red robes. From then on it went down hill! In 1794, the whole thing was cancelled through lack of interest and ticket sales.

In 1788 it was quite difficult to get from town to St Aubin so the first omnibus service was introduced. The route crossed the sands of St Aubin's bay.

Another first was in 1794. Until then, if you had wanted to post a letter to England, you would have taken it round to a local coffee shop, or perhaps to a merchant's office on the Esplanade. In turn, someone would have handed it to any ship's captain who called in. In 1794, the first official Post Office was set up at Mr Charles Le Geyt's house in Hue Street. He was proud to be Jersey's first Post Master. In 1851 Jersey was used in a new experiment. The first Post boxes, or pillar-boxes, in the British Isles were installed. One of them still stands today, patiently accepting your letters in the Central Market.

The French revolution, greeted with glee by The Gazette, saw a flood of French aristocrats arriving in the Island. We also received some three thousand Priests who had refused to take the oath of loyalty to the constitution. In all there must have been around ten thousand refugee/immigrants. St Helier grew. Builders made a nice profit, as did the boatmen who ferried the poor souls across the water.

A scam that was not appreciated was bringing French cows to the Island and then selling them on to England as being Jerseys. Jersey cows could be sold without restriction in England, but there was a large import duty on French beasts. The States soon put a stop to this lark. Anyone landing French cattle in the Island would be fined. His ship would be confiscated, whilst the animal would be butchered and distributed to the poor. This eventually led to the Jersey cow becoming such an exclusive breed.

It is interesting to note that there is an Ingouville Place in St Helier and an Ingouville Street in 'The old ship yards' in Sydney, Nova Scotia. Both commemorate the same prominent merchant family. Around 120 years later, an Ingouville was the first Jersey man to win the Victoria Cross.

In 1792, people of many nationalities were offering tuition in languages, singing, writing, acting and every musical instrument from flute to bassoon. 'Brute' Jersey was becoming civilized!

As the 18th Century lurched to an end, a hurricane swept across the Island taking the roof off a de Carteret house and leaving it two miles away. Louis the XVI lost his head, literally. Methodist Militiamen protested about drilling on a Sunday. A curfew was imposed on all foreigners. Another war with France was imminent.

CHAPTER EIGHT
1800 - 1900

Again the French had plans to attack the Channel Islands. An army of 20,000 men assembled in St Malo, intent on hitting all the Islands simultaneously. The idea was land, disarm the inhabitants and requisition all the horses. Their plans were meticulous, but it was a nonstarter.

In Brittany, disenchanted with the new Republican Government, bands of Bretons were forming an underground resistance. A young Jersey naval officer, Philippe d'Auvergne, was in charge of a flotilla of gunboats protecting the Islands. When Whitehall realised that the Breton resistance movement was spreading to Normandy, they were delighted. D'Auvergne was ordered to organize the supply of arms and ammunition. The work was exceedingly dangerous. It was also very difficult, as he was dealing with an undisciplined mixture of aristocrats, priests, women, smugglers and rogues. He named them 'La Correspondance' and somehow, kept them all headed in the same direction. Despite regular enemy patrols around the coast, he and his men managed to smuggle in vast quantities of arms and money.

Admiral Philip d'Auvergne during the French Revolution in 1789.

On one occasion, he received from London a consignment of one thousand double-barrelled guns and forty thousand cartridges. This was followed by a gunpowder and sabers cargo. Every last item reached the rebels safely. Young d'Auvergne's spy network was also legendary. Information was being gathered and passed on to Whitehall. There is no doubt that it was his brave efforts that kept the French too busy to attempt an invasion of our Islands.

By 1801, the war was running out of steam. Napoleon wanted peace and England was tired of it all anyway. Hence the Treaty of Amiens was signed. During the brief respite, just because we had occasionally attacked his ships, Napoleon made several hurtful remarks about Jersey. He suggested that Jersey harboured assassins and firebugs. We were a nest of brigands, traitors and vermin. In fact we were the shame of England.

It was war again in May 1803. This time it lasted for twelve years. Jersey's Lieutenant Governor, General Gordon proposed that the Island should come under martial law, a move that would supersede the Civil Courts. The Islanders were furious. Hundreds thronged to the Royal Square to make their feelings known. For the only time ever, the States met on a Sunday. General Gordon's proposition was thrown out by 26 votes to 10. Those ten were not forgotten. Threats were made and effigies were burnt.

The British Government decided to buy the Town Hill, where Fort Regent now stands, and fortify it. Up until then it had been a place to graze cattle and stroll about enjoying the view. With the help of workmen from all the parishes, an impressive network of trenches and earthworks were dug out. The only actual building was the powder magazine.

On June 4th 1804, a great crowd assembled on The Hill to watch the hoisting of the Royal Standard and the firing of a salute in honour of the King's birthday. No one knew how close he or she was to disaster! A short time later, the signals officer, Philippe Lys noticed smoke coming from the powder magazine. Whilst most of the soldiers ran for their lives, the signals officer, a Private Penteney and a carpenter named Touzel, rushed through the thickening smoke into the magazine.

After the Royal salute, a gunner had put a 'match', (a length of rope soaked in nitre, used for firing the guns) back in the magazine still smouldering. This in turn had set fire to a pile of matches. As they reached the fire the three horrified men could see that some of the gunpowder barrels were already charred and smoking. Quickly they flung the burning matches out of the door and extinguished the fire. It is thought that had the powder magazine blown, it would have taken half of St Helier with it! These brave men were given gold medals, 5000 Livres and a pension, which is still paid to their descendants.

In 1806, the foundation stone of the present Fort Regent was laid. The whole project was completed in eight years and named after The Prince of Wales, who later became George IV.

In the Parade Gardens, there stands a modest statue of General Don. The General achieved so much in his time as Lieutenant Governor, that he deserves a much finer monument. First he set up a system of signalling which would warn of a French attack. Look out ships were stationed in positions from where they could flash a message to Mont Orgueil. From there the news would be signalled to Grosnez and passed on to Sark and Guernsey, where the British fleet were at anchor. His system was tested and, amazingly, if the French fleet had left St Malo or any port along that coast, it would have been known in St Peter Port just fifteen minutes later!

The General also took the Militia in hand, moulding them into an efficient fighting force.

The system of Jersey roads was appalling. They consisted of exceedingly narrow lanes winding in all directions. The very high banks meant that during the wet season they became impassable mini-rivers, which was useless for the rapid movement of troops and guns. Here was another challenge for General Don. Proper roads were essential.

It was a costly and difficult exercise to build new roads throughout the Island. Trees were felled, farmland was invaded, even old out houses that impeded progress had to go. This was not always popular with the occupiers! One elderly farmer threatened to 'shoot the first man to remove a sod'! The General in full uniform picked up a spade and dug through the bank. No shot was fired and the old sod was removed.

Roads from St Ouen to Beaumont and St Aubin to town were just some of the eighteen that were constructed. This was despite a 'Clameur de Haro' (a prayer to 'Our Prince' which, by law, puts a stop to the infringement of property till the Courts decide the rights and wrongs.) A Rector condemned the work. Preaching from the Text, he thundered, 'The broad road leadeth to destruction'!

Knowing that during war Jersey could run short of food, this amazing man turned farmer! He grew several crops successfully on what was considered to be barren land at St Brelade.

Meanwhile Philippe d'Auvergne had continued to run his network of spies in France, but not for long. Napoleon himself now turned his hand to counter-espionage. He issued precise instructions to his secret police. Gradually d'Auvergne's network began to crumble and his most trusted agent, Prigent, was caught. He informed on anyone and everyone whom he had contacted or who had sheltered him. This of course condemned them all to death. He was trying desperately to save his own skin, but he was shot anyway.

As usual, if Jersey men didn't have a common enemy to unite them, they fought amongst themselves! After Napoleon had been sent on his holidays, two-party politics raised its ugly head in the Island. The two parties concerned, The Laurels and The Roses, hated and despised each other. A Laurels man would never allow roses to grow in his garden and visa-versa.

The Laurels faction attacked an Inn where The Roses were dining and, at the elections, which were not secret ballots, anyone voting for The Rose party was beaten, kicked and his clothing torn. So it dragged on and on.

Of course it was not all politics, people had to make a living. Agriculture and horticulture were of prime importance. The Jersey Cow was gradually coming into it's own due to the efforts of Colonel Le Couteur. He inspired the farmers to set up a selective breeding programme. Jersey milk gained in reputation and England began importing up to 800 Jerseys annually. Originally these animals were black, white or fawn, but when it was found that the fawn cows produced the best milk, the white and the black animals were bred out. An average of 30,000 tons of the humble spud was also exported yearly, but something better was to come. The Jersey Royal was waiting in the wings.

Cider was also a popular export. A quarter of the Island was taken up with apple growing and every farm had a cider press. In 1839 alone, nearly 269,000 gallons of Jersey wobble juice arrived in English taverns. Another nice little earner was helped along by there being no tariffs or duty imposed on goods made in Jersey. Duty free leather was brought in from France, turned into boots and shoes then exported across the Atlantic, easily undercutting their American competitors.

The oyster trade had been jogging along nicely during the early 17th century. It became serious business in the 19th. It was established that every Islander had the right to dredge the oyster beds, but the Royal Court forbade such frivolity during any month with an 'R' in it! Up until now it had been just local fishermen engaged in the oyster trade but, around 1830, it became the oyster wars!

Several English fishing companies got involved. Some three hundred and twenty boats sailed in for the pickings. Hundreds of women were employed sorting and packing these fruits of the sea. Cottages were built to house this new population. Gouray Church was erected to provide English services for the new oystermen and their families. With each boat hauling in some 12,000 oysters per day, the Grouville beds were soon depleted. The French did not mind the occasional Jersey fisherman dropping in for a 'feed of oysters', but a fleet of English fishing boats was just not on. Warnings were ignored and, when three hundred vessels invaded French oyster-space, two French warships went into action. Lives were lost. A fishing boat was captured and taken back to France.

When the rest of the fishing fleet heard about this, every one of them set sail for St Malo. In a fierce and bloody fight, the irate fishermen boarded the French warships, released the fishing boat and sailed it back to Jersey. They left many of their comrades dead or in chains.

To relieve the situation, the States spent £4000 on new oyster beds. Everyone was warned not to touch them till they were 'ripe'. Naturally this was ignored and one hundred and twenty English boats set sail for the new beds. As they went, they jeered at the Constable of St Martin who was attempting to stop them in his rowing boat. He was rowing his heart out but perhaps without blue flashing lights and two-tone horns, he didn't stand much chance! Actually, next morning he did arrest two of the ringleaders! The situation continued to get worse until, finally the Lieutenant Governor called in the Garrison and the Town Militia. A few cannon balls later, a subdued fishing fleet crept back to port. Ninety-six Captains were arrested and fined. The oyster trade began to fade out and by 1863 it was virtually at an end.

Yet another profit making scam was smuggling. Local traders would buy tons of tobacco and gallons of brandy and geneva (gin) from France and sell it to the smugglers. These illegal cargoes were then landed in creeks or on lonely beaches along the English coast. One such fellow who observed this was Humphrey Oxenham. It was one o'clock in the morning when he spotted a smugglers' boat close in shore. He could see several horses and carts on the beach, so he went to investigate. On closer inspection he also saw, surrounding him, some forty brigands armed with cudgels! He was immediately knocked down with a violent blow to the forehead, and then they bravely began to lay into him with feet and clubs. A boatman, James Hudie, came to his assistance, probably saving his life. The Commissioners offered a reward for 'information leading to smuggling' or 'La Fraude' as it was known for many years. Many cunning tricks were employed to fool the Customs. Small rolls of tobacco covered in a thin skin and smeared with mud could easily be mistaken for a cargo of potatoes!

Sailing ships were always at the mercy of the weather and delays were an accepted part of life. However a Guernsey Jurat attempting to cross the channel to St Peter Port from Southampton had a disastrous time. First he was becalmed at Cowes, he was then driven back no less than five times by severe gales. In the end it took him three months to get home. The coming of the steam packet was a Godsend to the Islands and eventually tourism.

The first paddle steamer, 'The Medina', to visit Jersey arrived on June 11th 1823. It had been hired privately to bring a family and their furniture to Guernsey. Whilst there, they ran an excursion to Jersey. It was greeted with great excitement by the crowds and, of course, the Militia band.

By 1824, two rival firms were providing a weekly service from Southampton. Inevitably, competition caused prices to come down from the original 30 shillings, (£1.50) to half a crown (12 p) for a trip to England. As it became a daily service the 'Mail boats' used to race one another across the Channel. First to pick up the passengers from Guernsey to Jersey got the extra profit.

The coming of this regular, reliable service led to two events. First was a vast influx of passengers from England. By 1840 there were thought to be an additional five thousand English residents. The second consequence was the coining of the phrase - usually aimed at newcomers who complained. 'If you don't like it, there's a boat out in the morning!'

St Helier was changing, as was the architecture. Fine buildings in the Georgian and Regency fashions rather than the French style, were commissioned by the rich immigrants and well-to-do local merchants. Between 1825 and 1831, Waterloo Street, Bath Street, Belmont Road and Great Union Road suddenly appeared. These streets first saw the flicker of gas light in 1831.

Thomas Edge was the owner of Jersey's original gas works. Eventually he sold this modern wonder to The Jersey Gas Company.

Several churches and chapels began to reach for the sky in the mid 1800s. There was the French Independent in Halkett Place, and a Methodist chapel in Don Street. Later the Methodists built the Wesley-Grove in Halkett Place, then another in Wesley Street for English speakers. There was the St James Proprietary in St James Street. Not to be outdone, the Baptists, the Primitive Methodists, the Ebenezers and more, were building like mad, all trying to gain The Lord's attention. At this point the Roman Catholics emerged from a small upper room in a back street and built a modest place of worship in Castle Street combined with an Irish mission in Hue Street.

Astonishingly, in the early mid 1800s, no less than six newspapers printed in French and ten English papers were circulating in the Island. Some of these newspapers were very partisan and resorted to slagging matches. One described the proprietor of a rival publication as, 'A spavined, glandered, broken down, broken winded, bedevilled, old pettifogging hack!'

Harbour facilities were very inadequate. When the King's nephew visited in 1817, he had to scramble on hands and knees over rocks and seaweed. In 1837 they decided to build a proper harbour. The result was the Victoria and Albert Piers. These have since been engulfed by a massive reclamation project and massive indecision.

In 1834, the States had adopted the English monetary system of pounds, shillings and pence. The confusion was similar to that of the 1970s when the Islands went Decimal. Yet it was worse because liards, livres and sous were also still official currency! Converting from one to the other was involved and led to a lot argument when goods marked in livres were paid for in pennies. To ease the situation, the States minted their own money. The pennies were stamped 1/13 of a shilling whilst the English penny was 1/12. This was to prevent the sou in the Jersey man's pocket being devalued.

Young Queen Victoria paid an official visit to Jersey. Poets composed odes printed on silk and painters painted frantically. Costly, decorated arches were erected all over the Island, St Ouen had the most magnificent, but Trinity had four! As the Royal yacht anchored in St Aubin's bay, rockets soared and bonfires flared. Most spectacular, if unintended, was the huge furze fire that engulfed Noirmont Point! A pavilion had been specially built on the harbour. A bevy of beauties scattered roses at the Queen's feet whilst singing the National Anthem, led by a lad with a concertina!

Her Majesty was taken for a drive to Mont Orgueil and back to the yacht. The visit had lasted just three hours. To commemorate the lightening visit of 1846, a college was built. Six years later they built Victoria College.

Boat building was big business in Jersey.

St Helier Harbour with a modern steamship in berth.

Military Parade at Fort Regent.

South Hill.

Horse and Carriage at Lanes Paragon in Halkett Place.

A slower way of life!
Above:David Place.
Right: St Peter's Valley.

Country ways.The whole family would work the land.The children would help before and after school.

As so often happens, many of the newcomers, including several retired Colonels, felt that they should change the Jersey laws and way of life. They secured the services of Abraham Le Cras, a man born in Salisbury of a Jersey family. He argued that Jersey's claim to home rule was founded on chicanery and fraud. He was a clever speaker and could influence the layman with his rhetoric. He persuaded the Royal Commission to look into local claims to independence, they were not so easily impressed.

Making full use of the two weekly papers, 'The Jersey and Guernsey News' and 'Patriot', sponsored by his backers, he blustered that the English Commissioners had been bamboozled by the low cunning of the Islanders. Jersey, he said, had no more rights over themselves than did the Isle of Wight. They were only fit to pass bylaws regarding parish-pumps and taverns!

He also had a particular hatred for the Honorary Police. A 'black list' was published. It named all tradesmen who were members, and encouraged English residents to boycott their businesses. He made every effort to stir things up in Parliament, bombarding the Home Secretary, the Commons and the Privy Council with petitions. All he gained was a recommendation that an independent police force be set up. They also suggested that the Royal Court be replaced by three Crown appointed judges. Eventually Le Cras got tired of it all and took 'the boat out in the morning', leaving this corrupt little Island behind him for the moment!

In Broad Street stands an obelisk in memory of Constable Pierre Le Sueur, and rightly so. Until he came to office in 1845, the town streets ran with raw sewage. The health risks were enormous and the aroma was worse. With the coming of the new Constable, all this changed. A complete network of underground sewers was built beneath St Helier. Some grumbled about the cost, but anyone with any sense knew it was worth it.

In 1847 wages were pegged at 10p a day. All very well but the price of bread was not pegged, in fact it went up just about every week! The workers grew angry. The rudders were removed from two grain ships, preventing them leaving with their cargoes. In February, the States agreed to have bread baked at a special low price for working men. The Constable promised to find work for the unemployed on the new La Haule Road. Everybody was happy but only until April, when the States stopped providing cheap bread! When notice of this absurd decision reached the workers at La Haule, they downed tools and marched on St Helier. The angry crowd grew in size as they picked up men from building sites and yards along the way. In St Helier they were joined by indignant town dwellers and the cry went up 'To the Town Mills' and 'Cheaper Bread or Pellier's Head!' Pellier was the miller at that time.

The men smashed down the mill doors and started to make off towards town with two wagon loads of flour. Constable Le Sueur and some Honorary Police met them by the Robin Hood Inn. Jumping on to a wagon Le Sueur challenged anyone to move it. Grumbling, the crowd moved off. The crowd who had swiped the second wagon put up a fight, but when troops arrived order and the flour was restored. For a while the Robin Hood Inn was actually used as a temporary prison.

Everyone had been frightened. The States subsidised the bread once again. The Island's Constables increased parish relief. The rich and famous contributed more than £700 to Constable Le Sueur's relief fund.

Also in 1847, the Admiralty decided to build a naval station at St Catherine, and one in Alderney. Eight hundred workmen arrived from England and Ireland. The first arm, now known as St Catherine's Breakwater, was soon built, but this caused silting, a danger they had been warned of but ignored. Because of this the other arm from Archirondel was virtually a non-starter. The coming of steam made the whole project unnecessary.

1848 saw a big influx of refugees escaping from an epidemic of mini-revolts all over Europe and from Louis Napoleon.

In 1852, Victor Hugo a well-known man of words and politics arrived bringing his hatred of Napoleon III with him. He and his fellow Frenchmen never missed an opportunity to vilify young Louis. They then made a horrible blunder when they insulted Queen Victoria! The Queen had paid a visit to Napoleon. England and France were now allies over the Crimea war. This infuriated French socialists. Three of them living in London published an open letter to the Queen which, of course, was re-printed locally in 'L'Homme', the refugee weekly.

The letter said. 'You have sacrificed your dignity as a Queen, your fastidiousness as a woman, your pride as an aristocrat, even your honour'. Next day the walls in Jersey were plastered with posters. 'Have you read the insult to our Queen in 'L'Homme'. The Lieutenant Governor expelled the editors of 'L'Homme' from the Island. Victor Hugo had actually disapproved of the article but he still signed the letter protesting at their banishment. He, his family and the other thirty-five who had signed it were also expelled. Victor Hugo spent the next fourteen years in Guernsey.

The Laurel party was in control for years and blocked every attempt at reforming the Constitution. The Privy Council got fed up with this and issued three Orders in Council. Establish a police court, a petty debts court and a paid police force for St Helier.

The Royal Court refused to register these orders. 7,000 people signed a petition to throw the orders out and even the Laurels and the Roses were united.

After twenty months of negotiation, the Privy Council revoked the orders! The States then passed an act establishing everything the Council had demanded! Now it was 'us' saying what we would do. The rights of Jersey had been established.

In August 1859 Queen Victoria paid another visit. The magnificent arches were long gone. She landed shortly after the Royal Yacht had dropped anchor and decided to visit Victoria College. She probably enjoyed this visit more than the last as, apart from a hastily procured bit of red carpet and a few market traders lobbing flowers, all the pomp had been taken out of the ceremony and the wind out of official sails.

Just as we thought that our constitution was nicely settled, Le Cras came back. Twice in three years he got someone to stir things up in the House of Commons and ask question about the Islands. Meanwhile he sent petitions in all directions and wrote reams of pamphlets and demands. In the end, ignored by the voters, and turned down by Parliament, he limped from the fray forever.

During this time another eight churches and chapels had sprung up to give comfort to the faithful of many denominations.

The days of the street water pumps were numbered with the arrival in 1870 of the Jersey Waterworks Company.

1870 was also the year that, amid great excitement, the rail link from town to St Aubin was opened. Engines and carriages steamed proudly forth, regardless of high tides.

This year of innovations saw our first telegraphic link with the United Kingdom. The seas around Corbière became brilliant with light from the new lighthouse.

The decision to build a harbour by running one arm from Elizabeth Castle and another from La Collette failed miserably as great waves continued to destroy work at La Collette. The cost to the States was £160,000, a sizeable sum. In those days you could build a fine house with all the trimmings for £860.

Several privately owned banks operated in the Island. The States had taken the precaution of ordering banks wishing to issue paper money to seek permission from the Courts. Everyone felt secure and happy until February 1873 when The Mercantile Union Bank closed it's doors! They were short of £270,000; their paper money became waste paper over night. Josue Le Bailly, the bank's Chairman was a highly respected Jurat who had topped the poles at the elections. He had also been systematically robbing the bank and it's customers. He got five years. When four months later another bank closed, the crowds went mad. They besieged all the banks demanding cash. The landslide had begun. As more banks closed, so did old established boat building firms and shops. Even A. De Gruchy and co. was bankrupt. Large English banks, including London & Midland, who took over the debts, eventually rescued the situation.

Jersey recovered well from the catastrophe. More wealthy immigrants were spending their money in the Islands. Tourists were spending time and money as they enjoyed the balmy climate. Locals took in lodgers and holidaymakers.

Farming, still the mainstay of the Island was doing well. Jersey cows were making a small fortune for farmers. The price of a cow had risen from £6 to £400 in twenty years.

Potatoes had been around in a small way since 1772, but during August and September 1807, 600 tons of main crop were exported. The blight came in 1845. This, followed by several bad winters ,almost ruined the trade and the farmers. Then a St Ouen's farmer, John Le Caudey, got an idea. He wanted to plant on the warm, south facing slopes, use loads of guano as fertilizer and, with luck, they might get crops as early as April or May and beat the competition to it.

He encouraged other farmers to have a go. He opened his own store for packing and organised the export of 'the earlies.' The first basketful reached the London market in April 1859. The 'potato season' was launched. The exports rose to 4,000 tons and the grateful farmers presented John Le Caudey with an illuminated address (now in the Jersey Museum), a gold watch (retained by the family) and 150 gold Sovereigns.

In 1880, farmer Hugh De La Haye was visiting Le Caudey's store on the Esplanade, when he was shown a very large potato with sixteen eyes. Taking it home, he cut it into pieces and planted them on his land. The result was a potato with a very distinctive taste. The Jersey Royal had been born. Within ten years the exports had risen to 70,000 tons.

Again in the late 1880s new churches were on the increase. The influx of Irish workers soon swamped their little church. The imposing St Thomas's Catholic church opened its doors in 1886.

The De La Salle Brothers created a school at 'The Beeches' in Wellington Road. Maison St Louis was home to the Jesuits but eventually became the Hotel De France. Highlands College began life as a French Navel school in 1831.

A late arrival was the FCJ Convent, constructed in Val Plaisant in 1909. It has since moved to Grainville. In 1880 The Jersey Ladies College opened in Roussel Street. It became The Jersey College for Girls and in 1888 they assembled at their new premises, Mont Cantel. In 1999, they moved to Mont Millais, near Victoria College for boys.

All steamed up. The Eastern Railway engine at Gorey in 1890.

The old Abattoir site and Albert pier.

The Roebuck steamship built in 1897 hits rocks in St Brelade's bay.

Litigation was expensive and often unnecessary. This was a lesson the States learnt the hard way. In 1890 a French woman convicted at the local Criminal Assizes was found to be insane and pardoned by the Queen. The Bailiff, Sir George Bertram refused to release her until it was registered in the Court. The Lieutenant Governor, General Ewart went to the prison, pulled rank on the gaoler, released the poor woman and packed her off to France on the next boat. The cost of the ensuing litigation involving the Privy Council was £1,000 and the Bailiff was ruled to be out of order.

Who is in charge of a meeting when the The Bailiff isn't there? His Deputy or the Lieutenant Governor? Finding the answer to this problem, (presumably it's the Deputy), took four years.

When the property known as Overdale was bought to house a smallpox isolation unit, the land rights also had to be purchased. The Crown owned the rights and wanted £48. The States offered £36. Litigation! The States won their case at a cost of £600.

The party politics had gradually died out to be replaced by individuals powerful in both knowledge and vision. Experience in industry and trade gave them the insight and ability to help run their Island. Henry Durell and Philippe Baudin were two such giants. Baudin, whose bust resides in the Parade Gardens, instigated the use of the Ballot Box in 1891. The population was now 52,000. English was the main language, except in the Courts, where prayers are still said in French. The form of voting in the States in French abides today.

The streets became a little brighter in 1891 as lighting by electricity began to take over from gas.

Communication got easier when in 1895, the National Telephone Company installed Jersey's first telephone exchange. The first subscriber to advertise their advance into technology was Down's

Livery Stables in David Place. There phone number was 11! A little over forty-five years later, during the Occupation, the Central Exchange became, almost certainly, the first in the World to be powered by a steamroller parked in the garage and connected to a dynamo!

An appalling tragedy marred the last year of the century affecting all the Channel Islands. On March 30th 1899 the steam vessel 'Stella' was heading for the Islands with a full passenger list of Islanders on their way home and holidaymakers looking forward to an Easter break. As the 'Stella' neared the Casquets, a group of rocks near Alderney, the fog came down. Captain Riggs slowed to 12 knots but then increased to 18 knots (around 25 MPH). With no radar to warn of danger, he sent an able seaman to the bows to listen for the foghorn situated on the Casquetts. At first he heard nothing as the ship ploughed on, then suddenly he heard a tremendous bellow of sound seeming to be just above his head. His warning shouts were pointless. The 'Stella' was twelve seconds from disaster. At full speed the ship hit a submerged reef. Sliding across the jagged rocks it's bottom half ripped out. She continued on for almost a mile before slowing to a halt. With seawater gushing in, the 'Stella' tilted backwards and slid to the bottom. Boats were launched; there were acts of selfless bravery amongst passengers and crew. A stewardess, Mary Rogers gave her life to save a woman passenger. One young man saved his life by attaching a football to his lapel. Some passengers were in lifeboats, some clung to planks and debris as they drifted in the freezing waters on into the night. By the time it was realised that The Stella was missing and rescue ships finally located the survivors, many cold dark hours had passed. Seventy-seven passengers perished.

The inquiry that followed could not decide why Captain Riggs had not dropped anchor till the fog cleared. Some said it was rivalry between companies that encouraged him to race. The good Captain could not tell them. He went down with his ship.

SS.Stella

Jersey's first motorcar arrived in 1899. It was a 3 horsepower Benz with solid tyres. This 'Devil's Machine' was delivered to Mr Peter Falla of St John by horse drawn trolley!

The last 900 years have seen changes in language, attitudes, trade, and lifestyle but the unmistakable Jersey man lives on. He will challenge and protest into the 20th century, as we shall see!

Rush hour in front of the Royal Yacht Hotel!

The Royal Yacht Hotel and other modes of transport of the day.

CHAPTER NINE
1900 - 2000

It was 20th Century and St Helier has its first official Fire Brigade. Until now, a mixture of well-intentioned but confused and untrained civilians plus a few policemen shouting orders, had tackled every blaze. Now they had three Officers and twelve part-time firemen. Their equipment consisted of two horse drawn manual pumps, fire engines, some hose and a fifty-foot ladder. Training began! Their first call at 3.40 a.m. was to a hotel well alight at, of all places, Grève de Lecq. Amazingly, the full crew was 'in attendance' within forty minutes! It was 1905 before their new steamer; 'The Lord St Helier' arrived. The first motor fire engine, 'A Dennis', followed smartly in 1921.

The celebrations following the Coronation of Edward VII, on August 9th 1902, included floral displays and fun in the sun on Victoria Avenue. The people enjoyed it so much that they decided to do it again next year if it didn't rain. It didn't and the Battle of the Flowers was born.

In 1906 Samuel Falle became Rector of St Helier and Dean of Jersey. His forward thinking was responsible for the Eisteddfod in 1908 and the District Nursing Association and Maternity Welfare Centre. He was also founder member of the National Trust for Jersey. He was a far-sighted and busy fellow. Education became compulsory at a modest fee. For those who could not afford it, there was the prestigious 'Ragged School'.

Around 6,300 Jersey men served in the 1914-18 conflict. 179 were in the Royal Flying Corps. Two Victoria Crosses were earned. There were 862 dead listed on the Roll of Honour. Guernsey and the other islands sent 5,300 men.1,200 failed to return. 260 Frenchmen who had made their homes in the Islands were also killed in battle. Alexander Coutanche negotiated Jersey's contribution towards

The First Fire Brigade, on Victoria Avenue.

The First Battle of Flowers, also on Victoria Avenue.

England's war expenses. They wanted £275,000 per annum; he got away with a one off payment of £300,000. No wonder he eventually became Bailiff and a 'Sir' many years later.

In 1919 women over thirty got the vote and in 1924, they were allowed to sit in the States as Deputies. The first wireless licence was issued on February 20th, 1920, and in December 1929 the first talking picture, 'The Perfect Alibi', was screened at the Picture House in Don Street.

The second hand bus that chugged its way between St Helier and St Aubin spelt doom for the Railways. Noting its success, several operators set up small bus companies. These used to race one another to the bus stops. Jersey Motor Transport Co then came in. Out went the battered buses. By 1935 both the Eastern and Western Railways had run out of steam and closed down. In 1925 the Imperial Airways ran a flying boat service to Jersey and Guernsey. It sank through lack of support.

In 1931, a bi-weekly service was tried from Southampton but it never really took off and was abandoned.

Jersey Airways then came, every day, tides permitting. The 'Airport', complete with weighing machine, was West Park beach! In 1933, it carried 20,000 passengers at a cost of £3 to £5 each. Air travel and tourism were here to stay and Jersey needed an Airport. They began building in 1935 and the final cost was £128,000. The official opening was in March 1937. A year later it was Britain's second busiest Airport.

Agriculture was still the main money-spinner of the day with potatoes in the lead over toms in the race for the English market. Breton labourers arrived in droves to work in the fields and on the steep 'cotils'. Tractors and lorries gradually replaced the horse, but vraic remained the favourite fertilizer. It was free for the collecting.

Jersey Airways De Havilland Rapide lands at West Park, 1936.
Note the wind sock on the swimming pool.

Eighty-one years after naturalists discovered an unusual beetle in the rocky mountains of Colorado, these striped munchers arrived to sample the Jersey Royal. This could have spelt disaster for the farmers and the Island. The States voted 42 to 2 for compulsory crop spraying. There was uproar. Hundreds of farmers massed in the Royal Square protesting at the spraying and protecting of their crops. Amendments were put, speeches were made and the order was reversed - 33 to 16 against spraying.

So Jersey drifted along. Tourists brought colour to the lazy, hazy days of the thirties. The beaches were packed. There were dances at the 'Pav' and Plaza ballroom. Hotels thrived, more cars, coaches and lorries appeared on the roads. Over eight thousand vehicles may have seemed a lot, but compared with today, it must have truly been the time of motoring pleasure. The Island prospered, then Hitler struck.

As the war spread across France, hopes that Jersey would remain a forgotten backwater as in 1914 were shattered. Family decisions had to be made. Evacuate to the mainland and a new life or stay and hope for the best. Around ten thousand decided to leave. One family, who had spent the day waiting down at the harbour, changed their minds and returned home to find most of their household goods distributed around the neighbours!

Although they were formed as a local defence force only, the entire Jersey Militia volunteered to leave the Island and join the British Army. Jersey was declared an 'Open Town', unarmed, not to be attacked. On June 28th, 1940, the first bombs fell without warning on St Helier harbour. The area was raked by machine gun fire. Several civilians were killed and fires were started up and down Commercial Buildings.The Second World War had arrived in Jersey.

The air raid siren wailed just in time for the second attack. An ultimatum followed, surrender or else. There was nothing else. White flags and crosses were displayed. Alexander Coutanche lowered the Union Jack.

The Town Hall flies the swastika and Jersey is under German rule.

The Occupation needs a book alone to recount all that followed during the next five years. Perhaps these few memories of odd incidents from those days will capture the flavour.

Thousands of German troops with all types of weaponry arrived in the Island and soon many new rules were introduced. All traffic had to drive on the right. Luckily traffic was light, comprising mainly essential delivery vans and lorries, horse-drawn carts, bicycles and buses. So the change over didn't cause the chaos it would have today. The telephone connection to England was cut.

In 1941 Hitler issued a Directive which laid down that the Channel Islands were to be converted into "impregnable fortresses" and Jersey was slowly transformed with bunkers, strong points, and tunnels built with slave labour.

All radios were confiscated. It was a punishable offence to own one, but many were cunningly hidden away in secret places. One young man hid his in the kitchen oven. Only his father and a business colleague knew the location. One morning his father said, 'I dreamt the Germans came and found your radio - get it out'. The young chap argued but his father was adamant. Two hours later the German police arrived and went straight to the, now empty, oven.

As in any country or community there were some who would 'cosy up' to the enemy, either for gain or to 'get back' at someone. They were in the minority, but it was still safer to keep one's mouth firmly shut, even amongst friends. There were more who got involved in small acts of sabotage or information gathering, and some managed to escape by rowing boat. In all cases they risked beatings, imprisonment, deportation and death. The rest of the population just sat it out week in and week out hoping hungrily for victory and liberation some day.

Even in plain clothes the German secret police were very recognizable. On one occasion two of them marched into a St Helier menswear shop. ' We wish to be like Englishmen' they demanded. 'You'll have to be turned inside out for that' replied the assistant. Sensing an insult they barked 'What did you say'. 'I'll have to turn my stock out for you' he replied innocently. Actually it didn't much matter what English style clothes they put on, as they always wore hats with a small feather on the side.

To be out after curfew, 10pm in winter, 11pm in summer, was yet another offence. One young man was seen by a patrol and made a run for it. The bullet actually took the heel off his shoe, but he got away. Musicians doing 'gigs' out in the country parishes, either attached trailers to their bikes or carried their instruments strapped on their backs. But once the dance was over they had to peddle like mad to get home before curfew.

As things became unavailable, innovation took over. Hosepipe was used for bicycle tyres. Wooden soled shoes with canvas tops were manufactured locally. Sawdust fires or communal ovens cooked the meals. Sadly, 200,000 trees had to be sacrificed to provide domestic heating and to keep the bakers' ovens supplied.

Electricity was rationed and there were long black out periods. Sometimes a car battery rigged up as a reading lamp came in useful. An elderly man who had tripped and fallen, had his broken finger examined and set in his home. The Doctor used the light of a cigarette lighter to work by. Fish liver rendered down provided cooking oil and an appalling smell! A family clambering over rocks at La Collette, gathering limpets for the pot, found themselves working side by side with a party of German sailors. They were armed with buckets and engaged in the same task. Neither side noticed the other!

The V for Victory signs used to appear in odd places. Stonemasons worked one into the flagstones in The Royal Square keeping it hidden with sand. It can still be seen near the southwest corner of the square. On one occasion a local man came up behind a soldier in the street and slapped him on the back. 'Hello Fritz, how are you keeping' then 'Oh sorry, thought you were someone else'. The soldier walked on with a large V sign on his back whilst the local man disappeared, brushing the chalked V from his hand! A heavily chalked V on the saddle of a German bicycle also proved successful. Swastikas painted in tar began to appear on the houses of known collaborators and certain girls who 'gave comfort to the enemy'. The German response was quick. A party of soldiers went out at night and painted swastikas in tar on dozens of houses all over town!

After D Day, with no supplies coming in from France, the situation went from bad to worse. There wasn't an ounce of flour left in the Island, men were too exhausted to saw wood and there was no gas or electricity. After several delays the Red Cross ship, Vega, arrived with food parcels for everyone, except the German troops. Later cargoes of flour began to arrive. The Germans took to eating pet cats and dogs.

Liberation came officially on May 9th 1945, but the British flag was raised in the Royal Square on May 8th. After five years of the swastika, that is a sight I will never, ever forget!

The Bailiff, Alexander Coutanche (Later Lord Coutanche) and the Superior Council had spent five years walking a tight rope. The German Command would issue some outrageous order. The Bailiff and Council would protest, negotiate and usually get some sort of compromise. Unfortunately, to the population who knew nothing of the in-fighting and brinkmanship behind the closed doors of the Commandant's office, the lesser evil that the Bailiff had to accept was still an evil. The ill informed opinions of some that the States 'did nothing and were collaborators' could be ignored.

On more than one occasion the Bailiff treated the German Commanders to lengthy explanations of international law and the perils of breaking it. In many cases the disputed order was revoked. One such was the 20% reduction in the Island's bread ration because part of a German convoy had sunk in an attack by the RAF. The Bailiff quoted International Law and the bread ration was restored to normal. It was lucky that many of the Commandants were men of honour and correctness, in contrast to the Gestapo and SS fraternity.

The Channel Islands sent ten thousand, four hundred and eighteen of their sons and daughters to fight Adolf Hitler. Eight hundred and seventy died, including twenty-eight in concentration camps.

A German officer at Gorey Harbour.
Inset: German troops inspect a cannon from another age at Elizabeth Castle.

If you wish to learn more about this fascinating period in Jersey history, we highly recommend 'Living With The Enemy' by Roy McLoughlin.

Thus it was that, with the enemy gone, a political party, the Jersey Democratic Movement, sprang up. They demanded a full investigation of the States, the Bailiff and the Superior Council. They also wanted Jersey to become an English county and the States got rid of. At election time the JDM fielded twelve candidates. Only one was successful. By now most of the Islanders had a better understanding of the States' efforts on their behalf. We are Jersey and intend staying that way!

However, changes in constitution were still overdue. One was redrafted quite quickly. Before the war, to be eligible to vote, a man had to be over twenty and a woman over thirty. Even then they must be paying rates or taxes on a property over a certain value. Today, being over eighteen and living in the Island for two years is all that is required. The States also agreed to pay the Lieutenant Governor's salary and for the upkeep of Government House.

One of the most important bills in Jersey history, the Contributory Social Assurance Scheme was proposed in November 1949. It was defeated by one vote. The country parishes were against it and there had been petitions, meetings and angry debates. In May 1950 Senator Le Feuvre presented the bill once again. The debate took two and a half days, during which time near riots broke out in the Royal Square. Tomatoes were hurled at the police who, in turn, charged through the crowd, truncheons drawn. There were several arrests. When a crowd assembled in Seale Street, near the Town Hall, where the prisoners had been taken, the police made another baton charge. A policeman was slightly injured by the swinging truncheon of a colleague! This time the law was adopted, but those who had voted 'Contre' made Senator Le Feuvre's life a misery from then on. Fifty years on, there are many of us who feel very grateful to the Senator as we receive our monthly pension!

Between 1948 and 1950 a series of disastrous fires broke out at commercial premises, mainly in the town area. An arsonist was at work. Martlands stores were attacked three times. Le Gallais, Huelins and Norman Ltd. were just a few of the fifteen shops and warehouses that were set alight. The exhausted firemen battled on. One night whilst fighting a fire on Commercial Buildings, half the crew had to be rushed to another blaze on the Esplanade. Firms began employing 'fire watchers'. Two detectives from Scotland Yard helped with investigations. Suddenly, it stopped. No one was ever arrested.

A treat was in store for motor racing enthusiasts when an international road race was planned to take place on a circuit comprising Victoria Avenue and the Inner road. The first race took place on May 8th 1947 with cars from England and the Continent competing. Unfortunately, at the third meeting in 1949, Mr K.W. Bear crashed his Bugatti at Bel Royal corner, killing himself, a Doctor and a Police Sergeant. That and the inconvenience caused by road closures waved the finishing flag on Jersey's International Road Race.

In 1949 another law changed, divorce became legal.

The building of new schools, homes for the elderly and flats and estates was the order of the day. The community was growing and public utilities grew with them. Fifteen thousand motor vehicles began to cause a bit of congestion and the crime rate was soaring. At least the paid police could operate anywhere in the Island. No more waiting for a parish Constable to give permission to cross his border! The Jersey Militia ended in 1954, a force that had defended the Island since 1336. Both the 'Morning News' and 'Les Chroniques' folded up in the Fifties leaving the 'Evening Post' as the sole newspaper. In 1962, Channel Television brought news, views and advertising to most households, in black and white. It was another twelve years before the coming of colour.

The complications of entry, or not, into the Common Market gave rise to endless discussions and meetings, both in the States and at the Home Office. Full membership would have effectively taken away Jersey's right to self-government, especially as Brussels had issued over three thousand edicts in just one year. Non-entry, on the other hand, would make us outsiders, unable to trade freely with Great Britain. Four years later a compromise was reached. Free movement of goods but conditions of employment must be the same as the EEC. The vote was 51 to 1 in favour of it.

Although Agriculture was still important to the Island, tourism had taken over as the main money-spinner. Coaches and pre-booked cabs provided by hotels and holiday camps lined up to meet holidaymakers at the harbour and the airport.

Hotels and guesthouses were usually well booked up. Anyone with a couple of rooms to spare in their home became unregistered guesthouses. The money was good and many long lasting friendships were made.

Many hotels held dances and cabarets. Two venues held six 'crazy-nights', sometimes advertised as krazy-nites, every week. These were a mixture of dancing, games and competitions. Indeed up into the 'Eighties', sunny Jersey was the place to be. Over one and quarter million visitors thought so in 1977. They spent more than £70M and not one could be persuaded to 'stay at home and send their money by post'!

Gradually, the cost of travelling to the Islands became higher and flying 'long haul' to far off exotic places became cheaper. The tourism boom began to decline. However, in 1992, nearly three quarters of a million basked in the sun, and if you walked down King Street at the height of the season, you were still likely to be trampled under foot!

As Tourism had usurped agriculture as the big earner for the taxman, the Finance Industry gradually came to the fore. In 1961 there was one merchant bank operating in the Island - Hill Samuel.

Thirty-eight years later there were over eighty. They employed around ten thousand people to look after ninety-six and a half billion pounds in deposits plus investments of thirty-five billion! Eventually the problems of keeping out dirty money and complying with the 'Proceeds of Crime' law turned bankers into unpaid policemen. They were liable for prosecution if a 'wrong un' slipped in through the net. The task was made more formidable by the 'Regulations of Undertakings' law, which made it very difficult for any business to employ extra staff not resident in the Island for five years. This was part of a 'master plan' to hold down immigration, but it put unnecessary pressure on the existing workforce.

One of the worst episodes in Jersey history began in November 1957. In a series of incidents three women were attacked in the Mont à l'Abbé district. One was raped and one escaped with knife wounds. This was the start of what became the Beast of Jersey's reign of terror. Over the next eleven years twenty-one women, young girls and boys were attacked and raped, mostly at the weekends.

In many cases the children were taken from their beds at night and led, often with a rope around their necks, across the fields. Strangely, the attacker always brought them back to their homes, sometimes even back to their beds, before disappearing into the night. Often he terrified them into silence, telling them to keep quiet and go to sleep or he would shoot their parents.

A women was left tied to a chair and gagged whilst the intruder, who had first cut the telephone wire, took her fourteen year old daughter out into the fields.

An airhostess, who accepted a lift, was half strangled with a rope, blindfolded and dragged into a field. She was taken back to the car but, as they drove off, she managed to free her hands and move the blindfold. As she opened the rear door the interior light came on. Startled, the rapist looked back, their eyes met briefly, and then she hurled herself from the car. Eleven years later she was still able to point out her attacker in Court.

Although a huge manhunt was underway, ancient laws hindered the St Helier paid police. They could not operate in any other parish without permission of the Constable of that parish! Unfortunately also when the children who had been abducted and returned told their parents, the parent's first reaction was to say it was 'probably a nightmare'. This of course resulted in delays in calling the police and cold trails for them to follow.

An almost unbelievable incident occurred when a woman who was walking alone was suddenly grabbed from behind, the 'Beast's' usual method. Just managing to turn her head, she recognized the man immediately; they had known one another for years! He ran off and, incredibly, for whatever reason, she didn't report the attack!

By now the attacks numbered sixteen and Scotland Yard had loaned Superintendent Jack Manning to the Jersey police.The Super decided that a massive undercover surveillance should be set up over a weekend in the East of the Island. As there were not enough paid police available for a job of this size, he approached the parish Constables. As each parish has several Centeniers, Vingteniers and Constables officers, this promised a sizeable force of silent watchers. Normally none of them operated outside their own parish and the excitement of it all allowed the situation to get a bit out of hand - including a lot of loose talk before the task began! On the Saturday evening when Jack Manning arrived in the area of his undercover operation his heart sank. He was horrified to find cars belonging to the honorary' parked all over the place with no thought of concealment. Some even had their interior lights on whilst the occupants wandered about smoking and chatting loudly. Never before had this professional policeman encountered such a covert surveillance situation. One honorary did have the right idea. As the Superintendent crossed a field, the chap, who popped up from behind a wall with a shotgun, suddenly challenged him!

Suspicion had fallen on Alphonse Le Gastelois, mainly because he was an odd character. Unkempt, he wandered about at night and lived on his own in the area of the attacks. There are always types who have to find a scapegoat and persecute it. Alphonse was not guilty of anything, but his windows were smashed anyway. For his own protection the poor man got himself taken out to Les Echrehous, a group of tiny deserted Islands fourteen miles from Jersey. All it has are a few semi-deserted stone buildings. Here he lived on water and seafood. Eventually a television programme told the story of his sorry plight. A load of food parcels and a radio-telephone arrived for him.

When a sixteen-year old boy was attacked, the police had a cordon around the district, with dogs, within fifteen minutes. The boy's father was out searching the district armed with his service revolver. Again the 'Beast of Jersey' had melted away.

Over all the years, so far the only clues were, rough height, musty smell, two part finger/palm prints and two pubic hairs. Some 30,000 fingerprints were taken. There was no compulsion, only thirteen men refused to be 'printed'. Twelve of them were able to prove their innocence. The 13th man said the police already had his prints from the occupation, when he had committed a crime against the Germans. As this would not have been considered a crime in Jersey law, the chances of the prints being around twenty years later were extremely slim, but he was adamant in his refusal to give his fingerprints on these grounds. Someone then remembered a box up in the attic at Police HQ. It was crammed with old fingerprint records from the war. Scotland Yard checked for months but they only succeeded in getting the prints into two piles, a 'definitely not' and a much smaller 'maybe'. The 13th man had drawn attention to himself!

When a fifteen-year old girl returning from a disco was attacked and raped near her home, a pre-planned operation swung into action. Patrol cars rushed to the houses of the men on the 'suspected list'. Questions were asked and answered. At the house of the 13th man, what proved to be half-truths from both him and his wife left the police, who had no right of entry, suspicious but empty handed.

Tuula Hoeock, a twenty-one year old Finnish girl was found battered to death in a field to the East of the Island. By the time the paid police got there, the scene of crime had been ruined by the clumsy feet of people who, although not trained officers, should have known better. A bunch of keys, belonging to the victim, were later found trampled into the mud. Tuula had been seen getting a lift from a white car or van. Though nearly 3,000 statements were taken and 2,000 vehicles were checked, no one was ever charged. Had the Beast struck again, this time fatally? This murder case was re-opened in 2006.

On July 10th 1971, the Beast of Jersey, the 13th man, self employed builder Edward Paisnel was captured for jumping a red light. When a patrol car flashed him to stop he sped off. As they chased him at speeds of 70 mph the police guessed the car must be stolen. He drove through a garden, a compost heap and a hedge but was defeated by a field of tomatoes. He ran for it, with a policeman in hot pursuit. The police car had stalled on the compost heap. As the driver radioed for backup, his colleague continued the chase across lanes and fields and a flying rugby tackle ended the Beast's reign of terror.

When Paisnel was searched, a wig, a rubber mask and ropes were found. He also had sharpened nails attached to wristbands and his lapels. His home was a farm, large and sprawling enough to house him and his wife separately. They were estranged and half the time she had no idea where he was. During a search of his quarters, which was an office/bed-sit, police found a secret room and the clothing described by the victims.

In November 1971 he was tried by three Judges, presided over by The Bailiff, and sentenced to thirty years imprisonment. He earned full remission and was released from prison on the Isle of Wight on

July 13th aged sixty-six. He died three years later. Opposition to him being buried in the family grave in Grouville was fierce. Meanwhile his new wife, he married his long-term girl friend whilst serving his sentence, had him embalmed and kept in their flat! Eventually, 'The Beast' went to meet his master. He was cremated. For a full account of this macabre story, see 'The Beast of Jersey' - The Final Chapter, by Ward Rutherford.

In April 1965, the Island was in shock at the news of a plane crash near the Airport. The BUA Dakota was attempting to land in fog when it clipped a landing light post. It cart wheeled and broke up. Of the twenty-nine on board, the stewardess was the only survivor.

During a period of two years up to this tragic incident, thirty-one people were killed on the Island's roads.

The Mail boats, which had been the Island's link with England since the days of sail, were beginning to see more changes. The old 'Sarnia' was headed for the scrap yard. But at least the £80,000 she would fetch would help pay for the new 'Earl William'. A bit of a gap in the service occurred when, whilst The Earl Godwin was awaiting its overhaul, the Soldier Car ferry ran out of water outside St Malo. A committee of inquiry was told that the buoys and marking system were to blame.

During the late seventies, Jersey reeled under the most appalling weather conditions, flooding, blizzards, icy roads and snowdrifts. The winter crops were wiped out and the Island virtually came to a standstill.

Just to add to the joy, a strike of lorry drivers in the UK posed another threat to the Islands. Whilst cargo ships lay idle at Portsmouth, supplies ran low. There was even talk of food rationing and, for a while, local Dockers were laid off. Gradually, as agreements were reached in the UK, normality began to prevail on all fronts, including the weather front!

During the Seventies there were proposals and debates about the introduction of work permits to limit immigration in Jersey. In 1999 they were still discussing it!

Crime, especially amongst juveniles, continued to increase but the European Court of Human Rights still removed birching from the Statute Books. They decided that birching young offenders was degrading. Despite massive Island support for the birch in cases of vandalism and violence, the Islands were forced to abandon this deterrent. Hooliganism, muggings, assaults and threats continued seemingly unabated. Another problem was French school children seemed to think that a daytrip to Jersey included the right to shoplift everything in sight! The once safe streets of St Helier were becoming a jungle. They didn't always win. When a man in Bath Street grabbed from behind a chambermaid in her early twenties, she punched him in the face and kicked him. There was a patch of blood left on the pavement to demonstrate his ill-advised action! There were calls for more police on the beat. Over the years, more police did pound the beat, but calls for more were still to be heard in 2006!

A rape at knifepoint and three attempted rapes all in a matter of days in St Helier had the already stretched police force on full alert, but in little over a week the crimes were solved. They never happened! The four girls, including the 'rape at knife point', had made the stories up. This was admitted in the Police Court. One got 28 days and one was remanded for the Royal Court. Four months later, it was decided that she could not be tried in the Royal Court. The crime she was charged with, wasting police time, did not exist, but it did very soon. In 1979, nearly 5,000 defendants appeared in the Police Court.

A bit of a storm in a helmet was blowing up between the paid police and the honorary system. The 165 strong Police Association told the Island Centeniers to decide if they are policemen or Magistrates. This came about as a result of proposals to increase the powers of the honorary police. Apparently the anomaly of a motorist being stopped, arrested by, and subsequently tried and sentenced by the same Centenier, was all too common. To add to their disquiet, the police still could not arrest suspects. They could only be detained.

Employment was high in the seventies but, as unemployment began to rise, Senator Norman Le Brocq attempted to introduce an unemployment benefit scheme. The scheme still hadn't started in 2006.

During The Queen's visit in August 1978, a scene reminiscent of the TV comedy 'Vicar of Dibley' was enacted. The Dean, feeling that he had been ignored, reported that he 'had to use his elbows' to force his way into a group of ladies who were talking to Her Majesty.

Tourism was very nearly scuppered in March 1978. The 100,000-ton super tanker Amoco Cadiz ran aground and split in two, just over one hundred miles away on the Brittany coast. An emergency meeting was called as the massive oil slick gathered strength and headed for the Channel Islands. Could it be prevented from reaching the Islands? How could we protect our golden beaches? The Royal Navy offered full support. It was feared that spraying dispersants on the oil could ruin the fishing for ten years to come. Fishermen, small boat owners, Aircraft and Department of Trade ships were all on stand-by as gale force westerly winds slowly drove the 250,000 tons of oil towards Jersey's shores. Locally, volunteers were ready to 'fight on the beaches'. The cost of preparation so far had been £100,000, and then it was all over. A massive spraying operation off the Islands did the trick. It cost the British Government around £1M. Jersey's share was £350,000. Guernsey paid the same. The French blamed the Captain of the Amoco Cadiz!

Ever since the 1920s, some one in the Houses of Parliament has been glaring at Jersey and muttering about 'low tax' and 'tax havens', then making silly statements 'in the House' or running to the papers.

In 1978, the Labour party sent people to investigate our 'Feudal System' and tax system. Again they recommended we become an English county. We did have some support from a Conservative MP, and the Bailiff pointed out that Jersey's Autonomy had been earned by service and loyalty. That kept them quiet for a while but it was an on going, regular gripe continuing into the 90s!

In the mid 1970s, the great Queen's Valley debate began. The Island needed more water but conservationists campaigned to save the valley. As a compromise, it was decided to build a pumping station to drain water from the valley rather than build a reservoir. A debate followed and it was again recommended that the valley should be flooded. This was backed by the T & G W Union whose members desperately needed the work. A group of shareholders in the Jersey New Waterworks Co. attempted to wreck the project using their 30% share holding. The Chairman of the JNWC, Mr Oscar Laurens, warned against a takeover by this group and asked for the support of the other shareholders. There were changes on the JNWC board and another change of heart, a new desalination plant? That would cost the Island a lot of money plus £400,000 a year afterwards. The reservoir would be cheaper and last longer. The National Trust for Jersey then refused to sell their bit of Queen's Valley. Compulsory purchase was on the cards. A referendum was on the cards. Now it was the turn of Grouville Parish to dig its heels in and refuse to allow the flooding of their valley. In 1982 it was decided! There was overwhelming support from the States. A reservoir would be built, despite protest marches led by TV 'greenman' David Bellamy. The delays had cost the Island an extra £6M. It was completed in 1991. Beautifully landscaped, it provides an excellent walk of about a mile. It is a home for many species of bird and waterfowl and 260 million gallons of much needed water.

Professor Grant expressed fears about the nuclear industry at Cap de la Hague. He said that Jersey was definitely within the French Nuclear zone and that their site contained some very hazardous pieces of plant.

His comments were borne out when a major catastrophe, caused by a fire, was narrowly averted. Cap de La Hague was within two hours of an explosion and a cloud of radioactive gas! The Defence Committee criticized the French authorities for not keeping the Islands informed. The French response was that there was nothing to fear and they gave a glowing report about the safety of their plant. This was to be an ongoing saga of reports, denials, rumours and fears expressed by Greenpeace from the 1980s onward!

Still in the 1980s, the Art Centre finally found a home in Phillips Street. The building was offered by the Education Committee on a ninety-nine year lease at a ground rent of £1 per year. The States granted them £250,000 towards the cost of building.

Meanwhile, there were worries that cutbacks ordered in the Public Health sector might curtail some patient services, including the Ambulance Service.

Unemployment continued to rise, Tourism continued to decline. Striking French fishermen blockaded the port of St Malo, leaving Jersey-bound passengers stranded.

Predictably boring, two Labour MPs attacked the Islands as tax havens that, presumably, should be towed out into the Atlantic and sunk.

After twelve years of careful consideration, and a final debate lasting over three hours, the States decided to accept the BBC's offer to set up a radio station in the Island. BBC Radio Jersey began transmitting in March 1982. In May 1986, it was proposed that States sittings be broadcast live. Now the thrills and excitement of listening to keenly honed argument and masterly decision-making was ours at the flick of a switch!

Nine people were injured in an explosion at the gasworks. Firemen and gas company employees, some with severe burns, were admitted to hospital. A leaky valve caused a major spillage of petroleum gas, which ignited into a fireball. Two firemen who had caught the full effect of the blast were rushed to hospital in a police car, which used the Queen Street and King Street pedestrian precinct as the fastest, most direct route!

The dangers of even an empty petrol container was demonstrated when a scrap metal merchant died in hospital having suffered 80% burns. He had been cutting up an empty 400-gallon tank with an oxy-acetylene burner when the petrol fumes exploded.

Several local service personnel saw action in the Falklands during the war with Argentina. When it was over, Jersey made a gift of £5M to the Falklands to help in restoration. Making this donation resulted in an unusual twist. The British Government smelt money! A contribution to defence from Jersey would be most acceptable.

It was time for debate, questions and letters to the Evening Post. Give them cash? Buy a Mine Sweeper? Get a Rescue Helicopter or ignore them until they forgot about it! In the end, the Jersey Field Squadron was set up. It was a bit of a cross between the old Militia and the Territorial Army. It was manned by local men and women trained by the British Army. The equipment was paid for by Jersey but not for the defence of the Island. The lesson was learned in 1940 that the Islands could not be defended. There were many scoffers but the field unit eventually proved to be very efficient. They were considered by the British Army to be a highly trained professional unit.

In the mid 1980's, tourism seemed to be 'on the up' again. A new daily roll-on-roll-off ferry service operated by C.I. Ferries was brought into service, carrying five hundred passengers plus cars. Cheaper package holidays were on offer.

A mark of the Island's popularity was demonstrated on Battle of Flowers day when a gang of professional pickpockets descended on the Island and lifted in excess of £2,000!

Another result of a bumper season was an announcement by the Constable of St Helier that 'bare chested men and bikini clad women would be discouraged within the ring road'.

Another boost for Tourism was the completion of Jersey Zoo's new shop and information centre plus an enclosure for ruffed lemurs. The German Underground Museum also added more items of interest to attract the tourist.

It was also announced that, under a new grading system, every hotel in the Island would have to offer a private bathroom or shower attached to every bedroom. Also the minimum size of a bedroom must be no less than 70 sq. ft per person. Expensive building work would have to be undertaken. In turn this would increase the cost to the holidaymaker. The cost of building work to extend the tourism office at the Weighbridge was found to have increased by 60%. This disturbed the Finance Committee. They were unable to understand it but, as any action might result in further costs, they could do nothing about it.

The BBC, on location in Jersey, filmed the Bergerac TV series. It depicted actor John Nettles as Sergeant Jim Bergerac, the Jersey Detective with a drink problem. The series was a great success and, by being screened all over the world, including China, it brought in quite a few tourists. Jersey people living in south Australia were surprised to recognize friends from 'home' who were extras in several episodes. In September 1985, John suffered a broken leg in an argument with a hire-car and the final episode had to be postponed.

Drug offenses continued to rise. The figure for 1986 doubled that of previous years. The new Chief of Police said that people needed to be more conscious about crime. He added that there would be less crime if the public were more vigilant and reported anything suspicious to the police. A States Deputy was charged with committing an act of gross indecency with another man in the Weighbridge toilets.

Three senior police officers had been suspended and charged with conspiring to pervert the course of justice and were then acquitted, but further charges were pending. The Dean was fined £50 for careless driving and over five hundred people were arrested for drunken driving.

Two ladies were engulfed in a sudden bank of fog while exercising their horses near Seymour Tower. They became disorientated and were unable to tell which way the land was. Knowing that the tide was rising, they headed for the tower. The horses were able to scramble up the approach and into the tower, but that was it, they couldn't scramble down again. Thirty-three hours later, with teams of volunteers working between tides, with mechanical diggers moving tons of sand and stone, a ramp was built. The frightened horses were led to safety by their tired but grateful owners.

Amid much protest and letters to the paper, using phrases like 'infringement of rights and liberty', a law making the wearing of seat belts compulsory was introduced. A year later, in 1986, statistics showed that the number of front seat passengers seriously injured in accidents during that time had dropped by 70%. In January 1985 computer users expressed concern that the proposed electricity supply link with France might pose problems when put into operation but they were reassured. Shortly after the switchover in May, the Island-wide power cut was less than reassuring. The JEC hurriedly promised consumers that cheaper power was to come by using the undersea cable from France, but they also decided to spend £5M on a new gas turbine, to act as a stand-by power source.

The Great Storm struck Jersey in October 1987. One hundred mile an hour winds lashed the Islands. Dozens of roofs were torn off and left scattered around the neighbourhood. Hundreds of trees were uprooted. Some crashed across roads to add to the chaos. Two children had a lucky escape when a chimneystack crashed through the roof near where they were sleeping. A falling tree injured a fireman. Those that had slept through it all woke up to scenes of unprecedented and unbelievable damage. Three days later, six hundred households were still without power and phone lines were dead. Ruined crops and smashed glasshouses added to the already difficult lives of farmers and growers.

As the Island took stock of the storm damage, the police had another problem. Elizabeth and Nicholas Newell were missing from their home in St Brelade. The doors were unlocked, the central heating was at full blast, but the house was empty. On October 11, they had dined at the Seacrest Restaurant with their sons Roderick and Mark to celebrate their mother's birthday. The couple were never seen alive again.

Roderick was an Army Lieutenant. Mark was a stockbroker. As a family they were not very close. Nicholas Newell was said to be a loud and rather arrogant man, likened by some to a typical Sergeant Major, but obsessed with money. His wife, Elizabeth, was more the sporty type. Both had been teachers. They seemed to be very close. The reason the central heating had been turned up in the Newell's house now became obvious. The place had been scrubbed clean but, despite this, police discovered minute traces of blood. The two sons were suspects, but there was not a shred of evidence to warrant an arrest. Five years after the disappearances, Roderick visited his father's twin brother and his wife in Scotland. Remarks he had made to family members previously, led to the couple contacting the police. When Roderick arrived, a tape recorder was in place. The confession was full and lasted for two hours. He told how, after they left the restaurant, Mark had gone to his own home, whilst Roderick and his parents went to their place. An argument had flared up. There were angry words, no doubt old resentments and past wrongs added fuel to the fire and Roderick told his father, for the first time in his life, just what he thought of him. A violent push sent Roderick staggering; he tripped and in falling hit his head. Near him, on top of a box of his possessions he had been sorting out, lay a pair of rice-flails. Roderick did not have much memory of what followed. Several blows to the head murdered his father. His blood had sprayed over the wall and ceiling. His mother was murdered in the bedroom. The savage attack left blood high on the walls. Mark's only involvement was after he had responded to a desperate call from Roderick; he helped his brother clean up and then to dispose of the bodies. If he had called the police instead, there is no doubt at all that Roderick would have shot himself.

Both Scottish and Jersey detectives monitored his story but they couldn't detain him. There was no warrant out for his arrest! It came two days later after the recording had been rushed to Jersey. By this time, Roderick was on his yacht, heading for the Atlantic. He was dramatically arrested at sea by the Royal Navy frigate 'Argonaut'. They found the bodies buried at Grève de Lecq. The trial can be found in 'The Newell Murders' by Anthony Masters and Philip Falle. Mark went to prison for six years and Roderick was awarded a double life sentence but is now due for release in August 2006.

In 1985, United States Law Enforcement Agencies claimed that huge sums of Mafia drug money were being 'laundered' in the Channel Islands, but happily, a few years later, the same Agency awarded the Jersey Police one million dollars as a reward for their good work in helping to clamp down on the drug trade!

It was in 1985 that the idea of buying Springfield Stadium was first muted by the I.D.C. Although it was already a football field, it was owned by the Royal Jersey Agricultural & Horticultural Society and used for cattle shows. In 1990, the States offered £4M for the site, to be used for housing. This offer was unacceptable to the RJA&HS and they threatened to make a private sale. Eventually a price of £4.2M and a large parcel of land at Trinity were agreed upon. In June 1997, a fine sports stadium was at last in place ready to host the Island Games.

The farmers were not doing so well. The Agriculture and Fisheries Committee asked for £186,000 aid, mainly for dairy farmers. A month later the big freeze came. £2M worth of crops were ruined.

It was in 1983 that a call for a massive reclamation site to be used for housing was made in the States. From then on the weighbridge, the harbour and the area west of the Albert key were to be involved in the biggest building project, the greatest controversy and possibly the greatest confusion the Island has ever seen. A continuation of the tunnel under Fort Regent led to the £14M underpass linking a confusing Green Street roundabout with the Esplanade. The seaside of the Albert key was filled in with rubble, and the new Yacht Marina was filled up with expensive yachts.

What to do with the old Abattoir building? Where should they put the bus station? New ideas were put up and rapidly knocked down. Committees met and committees disagreed. Plans were made and thrown out as unworkable. As time went on, the biggest steam clock in the world appeared on the Weighbridge. There was much ado also about La Fregate Cafe, built to represent an upside down boat. The number of times the Millennium clock count down broke down are uncountable!

It was the early 1990s and motorists were indignant. The constable of St Helier, Mr Fred Clarke, admitted that the Parish had, knowingly, been fining errant drivers too much for parking offenses. He also said that motorists had been fined for parking in places where they had every right to park according to law. Investigations and calls for resignations followed. The Constable said he would be standing for re-election at the end of his term. The Attorney General warned that he would oppose Mr Clarke's re-election on the grounds of his connections with the licensed trade. Fred Clarke was chairman of C. Le Masurier & Co. This was a family firm, which owned more than twenty pubs and a large cash & carry wines and spirits complex, worth over £30M. Fred Clarke was overwhelmingly re-elected anyway! There was more bad news for the unhappy motorist. They introduced the 'breathalyser'. There were several new and confusing one-way systems, roundabouts and circulatory systems introduced. To cap it all, the Constable of St Peter came up with the idea of Green Lanes. Cars 15 mph only, horses and cyclists were to take preference.

Just as we thought the Channel Islands were safe from invasion by The French, a man from Caen did just that. Carrying a rifle and 260 rounds of ammunition, he cunningly slipped, undetected, through customs in Jersey and Guernsey. He landed in Sark and pinned a notice to the board at the top of Harbour Hill declaring that he was the rightful Seigneur of Sark! The notice explained that he was taking over the Island at noon. The Constable and a Vingtenier (honorary police) arrived and suggested that he stop being silly. He was silly enough to refuse, so he was arrested.

The bombing of St Helier was unintentional, the RAF assured us. They were supposed to drop paper petals as a final to the Battle of Flowers, but some of the bags containing the petals failed to open. No one was hurt, but car roofs were dented.

Joy at the opening of Jersey's new Postal Headquarters for a mere £8M, was marred by news that the cavern being built under Fort Regent to contain storm water was already £20M over budget and rising. Eventually when it was finished, it was the cost, not the waters that had risen. The thing had sprung a leak!

Another leak was in the Cantrade Bank. Police charged three men with draining away 26 Million US Dollars.

States sittings were not all harmony, sweetness and light at this time. Accusations were levelled. Apologies were demanded and refused. Senator Syvret was ordered from the Chamber.

There were so many 'items on the agenda',(The Waterfront project and the Marina, inflated budgets and over spending, housing, number plates for cyclists, traffic calming and work permits,) that confusion, and tempers, tended to run high! There were thoughts that with the number of difficult and complex matters being dealt with compared with even thirty years ago, a complete revamp of States procedures was urgently needed.

Fog struck on an August Bank Holiday. The Airport was the worst hit. At one time it was reckoned that 5,000 people were about, inside and outside the terminal building.

The controversy over the sculpture celebrating the Liberation was resolved. Philip Jackson had sculpted a maquette, which depicted figures releasing doves of peace. Somehow it just did not appeal to the public or the States, both of whom were contributing towards the £150,000 fee. However, in the end, all was peace and light. The figures are now waving the Union Jack outside the Tourism Office in Liberation Square.

After British C.I. Ferries were sold to rivals Condor and Commodore, BCIF were ordered to pay compensation of £500,000 to Poole Harbour Commissioners. This was because Condor and Commodore had axed the service which had previously run between the Islands and Poole.

Condor's new £20M catamaran hit a reef off Tasmania causing £2M worth of damage.

A massive rescue operation was launched on Easter Monday 1995 when the Channiland ferry Saint Malo carrying three hundred passengers struck rocks off Corbière, Jersey's rough and rocky south west corner. The RNLI lifeboats were launched, as was the fire service inshore rescue craft. A passing ferry and several privately owned craft came to their assistance as the badly listing Saint Malo wallowed in the rough waters. Passengers jumped onto rafts or into the sea. Several people were injured but, due to the courage and experience of their rescuers, not a soul was lost. Later the vessel was towed away and beached to await inspection and repair. In September, an independent inquiry found the skipper of the Saint-Malo, 'guilty of a reckless act' by proceeding at full speed through a short cut between the rocks. Subsequently a sculpture depicting two clasped hands was erected at La Corbière to celebrate the rescue of the 307 passengers and crew.

Condor had introduced their new £23M Wavepiercer, Condor 12, to the Islands, but as time went on they suffered delays and more problems. Passengers were not happy, especially the ones left sitting in their cars on the ramp as their ship sailed away!

Things came to a head when, after a year fraught with problems, the Jersey Transport Authority announced that it had received applications from two companies to run the Channel Islands route. With three to choose from, including Condor, the JTA and the States of both Jersey and Guernsey had much to discuss. Strangely, despite everything, Condor got the job back, for the next three years anyway. In 1998, they purchased the 'Havelet' as a bad weather backup.

In 1997, two Jersey men had claims to fame. John Searson rowed nearly all of the 3046 miles in the 'Atlantic Challenge' solo in 59 days. This was after his partner had to be taken off with back trouble. He broke the solo record for the Atlantic crossing, which stands at 99 days. This fantastic effort cannot be acknowledged as a record because he started out double crewed.

Eric Blakely, a TV reporter, was the first Jersey man ever to reach the top of Mount Everest. He faced some problems at the beginning and there were two false starts, but in the end, determination put him on top of the world.

In 1998, Home Secretary Jack Straw announced there was to be a review of financial services in the Crown Dependencies. However, he overlooked Constitutional Conventions and good manners by not consulting with the Islands first. Whether the 'strong protest' from the Bailiff caused him to lose any sleep is doubtful.

Senator Stuart Syvret had been 'ordered from the Chamber' and suspended for refusing to apologize after voicing an opinion. Now he launched a criminal investigation into the actions of the Bailiff, Sir Philip Bailhache and his Deputy. His complaint was in relation to the way he had been treated. The Royal Court quashed the lawsuit leaving the young Senator to possibly face a hefty legal bill!

Talking of bills to settle, it seemed that every States building project to go way over budget was considered the norm. In the previous ten years there was an overspend of £44M. Because it was a difficult design, La Fregate was £100,000 over budget. The Airport went over budget by £10M. The debt was written off. This was Jersey, the builder's paradise where everything costs 50% more!

Meanwhile, back in the real world, a minimum wage of 3.70 per hour was proposed and the States voted themselves a 65% rise, plus £8,000 per year in unquestioned expenses.

In January 1999,Condor was having bad weather problems again. Despite bringing in the traditional ferry 'Havelet', the fourteen-hour journey experienced by passengers was cause for strong criticism.

Strong winds may have been a contributory factor in the crash in Guernsey of a Fokker F27. The freight plane was making a special journey to deliver national papers, which had been accidentally left behind earlier in the day. Eyewitnesses stated that the plane seemed to suddenly lose power whilst coming into land and smashed into the side of a house. Both crewmembers were killed.

The Guiton Group, parent company of the 109-year-old Jersey Evening Post, merged with the 102 year old Guernsey Evening Press. This £27M deal formed them into one group, but retained separate Boards of Directors. The papers also remained independent. The move protected both newspapers from getting swallowed up by large publishing groups. The only other independent local newspaper, the Island Eye, which became the Island Times, came and went in the early 90s.

There was more 'sabre rattling' from odd bods at Westminster calling for our tax havens to be towed out to sea and sunk. We had grown used to this and remained happily buoyant, but now an attack came from another direction, the Germans! The German Minister for Europe had set his sights on 'Our dear Channel Islands'. He told BBC Radio 4 that the Euro was a step towards political union and the union would ultimately mean the demise of the privileged tax arrangements of the Channel Islands.

The possibility that millions of pounds in legal fees might be spent on a major court battle was predicted. A company, Le Pas Holdings, claimed ownership of St Helier's Foreshore under ancient Seigniorial Rights. The fact that the Seigneurs owned the rights to anything washed up on their bit of beach is fairly clear. Whether it extends to anything else, like reclamation sites, is what may keep the lawyers rich into the next Millennium.

The massive street party planned to see in the Millennium was off. The party, with a cast of thousands, was to take place in and around Liberation Square and the Weighbridge, over the Midnight hour and beyond. The States had granted £150,000 for the festivities but, with the costs already at £250,000 and rising, the party was officially pooped! The possibility of doing 'something special' sometime in 2000 was suggested.

The Island was appalled when a former Victoria College Maths teacher was charged with sexually abusing several boys over an eight-year period. He was sentenced to four years imprisonment. An inquiry was also held into the alleged inaction of the Headmaster and other members of staff when complaints were first made in 1992. This led to the resignation of the Head and his Deputy. A second blow fell when a popular, recently elected States Senator admitted importing pornographic videos. He was fined £200. When he later resigned from the States after a breakdown, he sent a cheque to pay back the salary earned whilst he was too ill to attend. His offer was not accepted and the cheque was not cashed.

In July 1999, the Islands trembled as two merchant ships armed with cannon sailed past, one of them within seventy miles of our quaking shores. Each carried several tons of high explosive ammunition, eleven hundred tons of fuel oil and enough plutonium to construct sixty nuclear bombs. They were on the way to Japan, but had this lethal cocktail been shaken or stirred, it could have proved to be the final solution. These thorn-in-the-flesh, tax-evading Islands might have ceased to be!

The Solidor Ferry had a problem of a different kind to usual. In July, three drunken passengers attacked and seriously injured the Head Purser, Philippe Robineau. The incident took place in St Malo when Mr Robineau refused to allow a Jersey day-tripper to board the Solidor 3, because of his extremely drunken condition. The Purser was taken to hospital in St Malo and his attackers to a French prison. As well as serious charges, they could be facing a life ban from travelling on the ferries. Meanwhile two trained 'Passenger Liaison Officers' travelled the St Malo route permanently to 'defuse any troublesome situation'.

Tourism in 1997 saw a total of around 682,000 visitors to our shores, including day-trippers and yacht owners. This was good, but only just over half that magical 1977 figure. In 1998, the figure had declined again. There were nearly 19,000 'registered beds' awaiting the holidaymaker in the year 2000 and only 11,800 by 2006!

With the population now standing at over 88,000, plus around 77,000 motor vehicles, we could soon grind to a halt..

There were all sorts of things bubbling away in the melting pot in mid 1999. Some had confusing names, but worrying intent. Outsourcing, which was getting the job done by someone else, even outside the Island, was one item of worry in both the private and public sectors. Saving money or complying with the 'undertakings' law were reasons given, but fears of redundancies were very real.

The fate of the favourite venue of dance since 1931, the West Park Pavilion, was in the balance. Refurbish or remove? That was the question. It was replaced with 32 luxury apartments priced from £325,000 to £895,000. How much?

Forty years after the event, it was suggested in the States that 84-year-old Alphonse Le Gastelois got a raw deal when he was suspected of being the 'Beast of Jersey' and exiled himself to the Ecréhous. Should he get compensation?

Seagulls were really becoming a menace. The lure of fast food was enticing them into St Helier in increasing numbers. Instead of nesting on rocks or cliff faces, they made their homes on rooftops. From here they would swoop down on anything edible with shrill cries. As they became bolder, anyone picnicking on the beach was likely to be mugged for their sandwich and no child with an ice cream was safe. They were bold and they were vicious.

The last eclipse of the sun to be seen in Jersey was in 1927. The next one is seventy-two years hence. The one we had on August 11th

1999 was virtually obscured by cloud. If you are reading this in 2072, I hope you get a better day for it!

The day after that spectacular non-happening was the last Jersey Battle of Flowers of the Millennium. As usual, it was packed to capacity. The RAF Red Arrows display team did their stuff and, true to tradition, the sun was shining down. The Battle had it's 100th anniversary in 2002 and it was one to be remembered.

That event, like so many in the Island was attended by the Order of St John Ambulance Brigade in their capacity as providers of emergency first aid. The volunteers of this organization have been doing their bit in this field for over 900 years, almost a Millennium of service to the community.

The year 2000 was marked with huge parties and each Parish erected a granite Millennium cross to mark 2000 years of Christianity. The Millennium park still hasn't appeared.

There was a complete overhaul of our government in 2005 and at midnight on 8th of December the committee system that had served the States since 1524 was formally abolished. The first meeting of the Council of Ministers took place on the following morning. Frank Walker made the history books, well this one at least, as being the Islands first Chief Minister.

If reading this has whetted your appetite for the history of Jersey, visiting the excellent Museums in the Island will give you food for thought. The award winning Maritime Museum also houses the Occupation Tapestry. Visiting the two Castles, Elizabeth and Mont Orgueil featured so often in this saga, gives a real sense of the past. Mont Orgueil's latest makeover costing £3.5m was finished in April 2006.

You could of course plan an assault on the battlements, as in the days of yore, but frankly it's easier to pay at the gate. Why didn't the French think of that?

Some other titles from Seeker Publishing

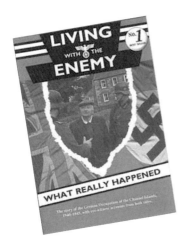

Living With The Enemy
First published in 1995, this book
about the German Occupation of
the Channel Islands has hit the
No.1 spot every year as the
best-selling local book.
Price inc. P&P to the UK £8.25

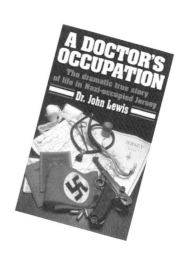

A Doctor's Occupation
First published in 1982 by Transworld
Publishers, this well known
Occupation book, published locally
from 1997, is still a firm favourite.
Price inc. P&P to the UK £6.50

Hitler's British Islands
From the landing of the troops in 1940 to the
Liberation 5 years later, these recollections will take
you through those dark years and explain how it felt
to be living in the shadow of a foreign power.
More than 80 Occupation photographs.
Price inc. P&P to the UK £5.50